Go ho

Manchester University Press

GO HOME?

The politics of immigration controversies

Hannah Jones, Yasmin Gunaratnam,
Gargi Bhattacharyya, William Davies,
Sukhwant Dhaliwal, Kirsten Forkert,
Emma Jackson and Roiyah Saltus

Manchester University Press

Published by Manchester University Press
Altrincham Street, Manchester M1 7JA

www.manchesteruniversitypress.co.uk

British Library Cataloguing-in-Publication Data
A catalogue record for this book is available from the British Library

Library of Congress Cataloging-in-Publication Data applied for

ISBN   978 1 5261 1321 4   hardback

ISBN   978 1 5261 1322 1   paperback

ISBN   978 1 5261 1794 6   open access

First published 2017

The publisher has no responsibility for the persistence or accuracy of URLs for any external or third-party internet websites referred to in this book, and does not guarantee that any content on such websites is, or will remain, accurate or appropriate.

Typeset
by Toppan Best-set Premedia Limited
Printed in Great Britain
by CPI Group (UK) Ltd, Croydon, CR0 4YY

This book is dedicated to all of those
who have lost their lives or suffered
as a result of racism and xenophobia,
and to those still seeking a home.

Contents

Figures

Thank you to the copyright holders for their permission to reproduce the images used in this book.

Every effort has been made to obtain permission to reproduce copyright material, and the publisher will be pleased to be informed of any errors and omissions for correction in future editions.

Notes on authors

Emma Jackson is a Lecturer in Sociology at Goldsmiths, University of London

For me, getting involved in the Mapping Immigration Controversy project was a practical response to the challenge Hannah posed on Twitter when we were discussing the Go Home vans – which was (paraphrasing) 'there must be something we can do other than talk amongst ourselves?' Sitting in Glasgow, where I was working at the time, I was watching the van campaign and the intensified raids in London from a distance, feeling far away and powerless to do anything helpful. Then the intervention in the UK Border Agency Glasgow offices sparked protest in my new city. So, I was motivated by anger and the urge to 'do something' but I also thought these campaigns raised important sociological questions about the place of border control and the use of emotion in governance.

A lot of what I do is about researching questions of belonging, spatial practices and how these are shaped or intersect with forms of power in urban contexts. In this project I've been particularly interested in how anti-immigration interventions feed into the production of particular spaces and places. It also relates to the work I have done with Hannah on emotion and location for our edited book *Stories of Cosmopolitan Belonging: Emotion and Location* (Routledge/Earthscan, 2014).

Gargi Bhattacharyya is a Professor of Sociology at the University of East London and co-director of the Centre for Migration, Refugees and Belonging

I met most of the other people on this project at an event that I organised on scholarship and activism against racism at the University of East London in July 2013. Out of this network, we organised a street survey to challenge the racist common sense of immigration checks in public spaces – I think because of this, I was invited to join the Mapping Immigration Controversy team. I have been so, so pleased to work collaboratively on these urgent issues with this wonderful group.

Hannah Jones is an Associate Professor in Sociology at the University of Warwick

I had been angry for a long time about the unfairness of migration control and public debate, but the Go Home van was a trigger for more concerted action. Inspired by the space Gargi had created at a workshop some weeks previously, at which we discussed how social research could be a tool for social justice, it seemed like the horrible moment of the Home Office campaigns could be used to galvanise us to use our research skills to try to shift these debates in some way. The coming together of a group of people who wanted to try out similar things was what made this happen.

In the past, I worked in local government policy and wrote my PhD about the ways that policy practitioners operate in what might be termed 'postpolitical' environments. This meant that one element of the project that was especially important to me was our attempt to understand how the people behind initiatives like the Go Home van understood them – rather than simply imagining the Home Office as a monolithic villain. More generally, my research interests in everyday racisms and multiculture, and in power and emotion, ran through the central concerns of the project – as did my interest, shared with the rest of the team, in paying critical attention to research methods as a form of knowledge production which is too often under-discussed.

Kirsten Forkert is a Senior Lecturer in the School of Media at Birmingham City University

I became involved in the project through the work I was doing with Action Against Racism and Xenophobia (AARX), where I carried out street surveys in Birmingham together with Gargi Bhattacharyya. I was concerned at the increasingly strident anti-immigration rhetoric from both the government and the media. As a non-European citizen and a racially minoritised person, I also found myself the object of both immigration legislation and anti-immigration rhetoric.

My involvement follows on some campaigning and writing I had done around the situation facing international students in the UK, about which a chapter is published in *The Assault on Universities* (Bailey and Freeman (eds), Pluto, 2011).

Roiyah Saltus is a Principal Research Fellow in the Faculty of Life Sciences and Education at the University of South Wales
I also attended the conference hosted by Gargi at the University of East London and became involved in the online outcry about the Go Home campaign. I was keen to explore the impact that the campaign, and the increasingly tough anti-immigration stance of the UK government, was having in Wales. As a female Caribbean migrant, I am part of 'they'.

Sukhwant Dhaliwal is a Research Fellow in the Institute for Applied Social Research, University of Bedfordshire
I felt frustrated by the mainstream discussion of immigration, the sense that an anti-immigrant position had become an undisputed norm across the media and main political parties. I wanted to be part of a research project that could poke holes in this newfound 'common sense' by bringing anti-racist research to bear, especially giving voice to local people who are being impacted by immigration policies. I also felt motivated by the research team, their political orientation and their mode of working, particularly their commitment to working collaboratively with civil society organisations.

I moved to academia after working for ten years in the voluntary sector, notably for feminist organisations challenging violence against women and girls. This project connects with my overall focus on equalities and discrimination. My experience in the voluntary sector in Britain has been complemented by an academic career that encompasses research projects on five out of six of the equality strands – 'race', gender, disability, age, religion and belief – including research projects about racial harassment in the public housing sector, racism and trade unionism, the intersection of race and disability in meeting the housing needs of Black disabled people, the work experiences of older men and older women, the impact on women of religious fundamentalism, and the impact of religious mobilisations on relations between the state and civil society.

William Davies is a Senior Lecturer in Politics at Goldsmiths, University of London
I was shocked by news of the Go Home vans and began to discuss the issue with colleagues, some of whom are co-authors of this book. One thing that immediately concerned me was whether those expressing liberal outrage might be unwittingly complicit in a communications strategy, that is, whether this apparent information campaign

might be more about image-management for the Home Office (for whom provoking liberal outrage is a badge of honour) than about the ostensible goal of achieving more voluntary returns. I was keen to investigate this more.

Much of my work has been on rationalities of policy-making and state strategy, especially on neoliberalism and the recent turn to psychological government (as exemplified in 'nudge' and 'wellbeing' policy). Migration policy is shaped by some of these rationalities up to a point. But this project also led me to investigate aspects of power that are not captured in studies of, say, governmentality. Often power works in a more contingent, affective, violent and visceral fashion than is apparent if one thinks only in paradigmatic ways. This project has pushed me to think beyond the theoretical and methodological limits that I've previously worked within.

Yasmin Gunaratnam is a Reader in Sociology at Goldsmiths, University of London

I was on research leave and working on migration and transnational dying and care when I heard about the Go Home vans. Questions of belonging, home and hospitality were very much on my mind and I had recently set up my first website for the work. Those two words 'Go Home' hit me in the gut. It was one of those moments when life seemed to swing in an arc, taking me back to a time of childhood and street racism. Now again, a more blatant, unashamed xenophobia seemed to be taking hold. There was talk about scarce resources being depleted by migrants, the term 'health tourists' was being bandied about. The first ever blog post I wrote was about hospitality and the Go Home vans. Emma Jackson and Hannah Jones got in touch with me through Twitter about the post and we began that conversation, 'What can we do?' A few weeks later I was on the High Street in New Cross doing a survey with a group of volunteers, listening to what people had to say about immigration.

I've been working for many years on the long shadows of colonialism and its entanglements with social exclusion. What was so appealing about this project was working in partnership with others. The team was a place of lively discussion, a hospitable space.

Acknowledgements

The Mapping Immigration Controversy project has been immensely rewarding and it has been a huge privilege to work closely with so many inspiring community organisations and activist networks, and to have had the opportunity to listen to the views, feelings and experiences of local residents across England, Scotland and Wales. This research project simply would not have been possible without the input of around a hundred research participants. We are indebted to these local residents and activists for their candidness, their willingness to engage with our questions, giving up hours at a time to provide the insights that have formed the backbone of our research findings. In each area we worked closely with and through a number of inspiring community partners who have persisted with their support work, service provision and lobbying as well as finding energy and time to input into projects like ours irrespective of this particular difficult period of immigration controls and anti-immigrant sentiments. In particular, we would like to thank Rita Chadha at the Refugee and Migrant Forum of Essex and London; Meena Patel, Sonja Kapalay and Pragna Patel at Southall Black Sisters; the Foundation for Refugee Education; Women Seeking Sanctuary Advocacy Group; Mike Quiggin and Bal Athwal at Bradford Resource Centre; Bradford Immigration and Asylum Support and Advice Network; Sunny Omwenyeke, Alison Graham, Saqlain Shah and Boniface Mambwe at Birmingham Asylum and Refugee Association; Dave Stamp at the Asylum Support and Immigration Resource Team in Birmingham; the Coventry Asylum and Refugee Action Group; the Hope Project; and Robina Qureshi and Sunny Singh from Positive Action in Housing. We would also like to thank Michael Keith for his help with access to policy officers who provided insights into the logic of immigration control and rhetoric for government. As a counterpoint, we benefited from rich exchanges with a number of activists and activist networks and we would particularly like to thank Margaret Woods at the Glasgow Campaign to Welcome Refugees, John Wilkes at the Scottish Refugee Council, Phill Jones at the The Unity Centre, Wilf Sullivan at the Trade Unions Congress, Suresh Grover at The Monitoring Group, Harsev Bains at the Indian Workers Association (GB), and Guy Taylor and Charlotte Peel at the Joint Council for the Welfare of Immigrants. In addition to those already mentioned, others helped us to organise local feedback sessions and parliamentary discussions that were vital for getting the findings out there. For this we would like to thank Gary Christie at the Scottish Refugee Council, Amal Azzudin, Janpal Basran at the Southall Community Alliance, and Don Flynn at Migrants' Rights Network. The original research proposal was developed in close discussion with Rita Chadha at the Refugee and Migrant Forum of Essex and London and supported throughout by a number of project partners and advisory group members who we wish to thank for their enthusiasm, energy and foresight in helping us prepare, plan and deliver a fast-paced response to a contentious contemporary issue: Alison Phipps at Glasgow University/GRAMNet; Omar Khan at the Runnymede Trust; Graham O'Neill at the Scottish Refugee Council; Jason Bergen and Nazek Ramadan at Migrant Voice; Ben Gidley at COMPAS, Oxford University and now at Birkbeck, University of London; Les Back at Goldsmiths, University of London; Nira Yuval-Davis at the Centre for Research on Migration, Refugees and Belonging, UEL; Nasar Meer at Strathclyde University; John Solomos at the University of Warwick; Sophie Wickham at Refugee Action. We were very fortunate to have ended our project with a wonderful interdisciplinary and collaborative conference and we thank the speakers, performers and participants for making it so inspiring, accessible and relevant. In addition to those already mentioned, we are thankful for the creative interventions of Alexander D. Great (who put our thoughts to music), Zodwa Nyoni, Maisie Tomlinson, and Hope Projects, and speakers Bridget Anderson, University of Oxford; Georgie Wemyss, University of East London; Hannah Lewis, University of Sheffield; Heaven Crawley, University of Coventry; and Alexandria Innes, University of East Anglia. We especially thank Samantha Asumadu, the Feminist Filmmaker, for producing a brilliant short film about the project that perfectly encapsulates the key messages from the research and has become a great resource for teaching and communication. Last but not least, thanks to Tom Dark at MUP for being an imaginative and supporting commissioning editor, helping us to put together an accessible and, we hope, engaging book so that we can make our research available and open to the wider world as well as the researchers, students and colleagues we hope will find it useful.

We thank and acknowledge funding from the ESRC; this work was supported by the Economic and Social Research Council grant number ES/L008971/1. We would also like to thank the University of Warwick Library for funding which has enabled us to make the online version of this book available for free and open access.

Note on terminology

The vocabulary used to describe ethnic, racial and migration identities is inevitably flawed and contested. In this book we have chosen to use some terms and not others:

Migrant – We use this term to denote those who have moved, either temporarily or permanently, from one country to another. In some research studies, the category 'migrant' refers to those who have citizenship in another country from the one in which they reside. We do not refer to descendants of migrants as migrants unless they themselves have also moved between countries, nor as second- or third-generation migrants.

Asylum seeker – Someone who has left their country of citizenship and applied for asylum (refugee status) in another country but whose application has not yet been decided.

Refugee – The 1951 Refugee Convention defines a refugee as 'any person who, owing to a well-founded fear of being persecuted for reasons of race, religion, nationality, membership of a particular social group or political opinion, is outside the country of his/her nationality and is unable, or owing to such fear, is unwilling to avail himself/herself of the protection of that country'.

Illegal/irregular – Rather than referring to an individual as an 'illegal' migrant we use the terms 'irregular' and 'undocumented' for those without a visa or citizenship as this is usually more accurate, given the frequent changes in law and its interpretation, and individuals' changing circumstances in relation to this. The exception to this use of language is when we refer to the survey work undertaken with Ipsos MORI. In some of the questions for that survey, the term 'illegal/irregular migrant' was used, as it was seen as more likely to be recognised in everyday conversation.

Minoritised – In general we do not use the term 'minority ethnic' or 'ethnic minority', except when this is the term used in texts we are discussing or by others we have been in conversation with (for the survey we commissioned, for example, Ipsos MORI use the language of 'white' or 'black and minority ethnic (BME)'). We use 'racialised minorities' and 'racially minoritised' to draw attention to the active processes of racialisation that are involved in terminology.

EU citizen – In most countries of the European Union (EU), citizens of fellow member countries of the EU are referred to as EU citizens, and migrants from countries outside the EU are referred to as 'third-country nationals'. In the UK, common political and public debate has tended to refer to citizens of other EU countries as migrants, despite sharing many similar rights of settlement, work and welfare with UK citizens while the UK remains a member state of the EU.

1

Introduction

To say good-bye is to submit to the will of heaven.
John Berger and Jean Mohr (2010/1975: 36)

'It's extreme, scary', said a woman from Senegal. She was looking at an image of a van carrying a government billboard with the words 'In the UK illegally? GO HOME OR FACE ARREST'.

Hannah had asked this group of asylum seekers and refugees in Bradford what came to mind when they saw the photograph of the van and its huge billboards (see Figure 1). For the next person to speak, it was the broken promises between a husband and wife. Imagine this, Sara[1] said: in their country he had made her many promises, now she's alone here, she doesn't know anything. She does not know about the rules. In this new world her husband is everything. Imagine that her husband beats her and kicks her out. She tries to ask her family for help but they will not let her come back: 'Where will she live? Where will she go?'

Lucee, a refugee from Sierra Leone, worried that the van would create 'racial tension'. All foreigners could be stigmatised. In the area where she lived, 'there had been a few racist things going on ... these are people who obviously don't care whether I've got my stay or not ... every time they've seen me they've always told me to go back to my country. So imagine if they saw this they'd probably call them [the Home Office], pick me up [laughs], do you know?'

The van had got Abas thinking about why he had fled Afghanistan to come to England, rather than seeking refuge elsewhere. In his mind's eye, England was a place where he might be able to continue his education or even get a good job; there was the BBC, and the best newspapers!

---

[1] All the interviews were anonymised to protect the privacy of the research participants, so the names used in this book are pseudonyms.

Figure 1: Go Home van

That a single image of a government immigration policing campaign can bring up such thoughts and feelings begins to suggest something of the emotional, existential and political textures of contemporary immigration control – the 'submitting to the will of heaven' – of which the crossing of national borders and citizenship rights is just one part. For those like Lucee, the Go Home campaign is frightening because it might inflame the hostility and racism that she has already faced in her local community. Sara's stream of consciousness is deeply gendered; the figures of an aggressive and volatile husband and a host country are almost interchangeable (see also Gunaratnam and Patel, 2015). The questions Sara asked in imagining a homeless and abused wife – 'Where will she live? Where will she go?' – when transposed into the contemporary political vocabulary of the nation state can be read as: Who belongs? Who can move and how easily? Who can stay? For how long? And on what terms?

It was questions like this that troubled us when we came together as activist researchers to counter the 2013 Home Office immigration publicity campaign 'Operation Vaken', of which the vans discussed in the Bradford focus group were a part. Five months later, and in partnership with civil society organisations in six different areas in England, Scotland and Wales, our funded project, 'Mapping Immigration Controversy' (MIC) began. We used multiple methods (ethnographic observation, focus groups, qualitative interviews and a survey) to research Vaken-related policy and media narratives and associated initiatives. We were especially keen to investigate Vaken's aftermath in local communities.

The moment of the Go Home van seemed to us to be a turning point in the climate of immigration debates – a ratcheting up of anti-migrant feeling to the point where it was possible for a government-sponsored advertisement to use the same hate speech and rhetoric as far-right racists. Sadly, as we finish writing this book in the immediate aftermath of the UK's June 2016 referendum on membership of the European Union, it seems as if the process has gone full circle. In the days immediately following the narrow vote to 'Leave' the EU, after a campaign largely focused on the 'problem' of immigration control, there have been many reports of physical and verbal abuse of migrants and racially minoritised people, linked directly to the Leave vote and to the violating language of the Go Home van. Shazia Awan, a Muslim businesswoman from Caerphilly in Wales and a Remain campaigner in the referendum, was told on Twitter the day after the referendum result 'Great news ... you can pack your bags, you're going home ... BYE THEN' (Staufenberg, 2016). Signs saying 'Leave the EU, No more Polish vermin' were left outside homes and schools in Hunting-don, Cambridgeshire (BBC News, 2016). Countless other reports of people – mostly nationals of other EU countries, and British Muslims – being threatened and told they must 'go home now' began to cir-culate in press and social media reports (Agerholm, 2016; Lyons, 2016; York, 2016).

Before the referendum votes were cast, in the midst of the cam-paign, the Labour Member of Parliament and pro-refugee campaigner Jo Cox was murdered in a horrifyingly brutal attack. Witnesses reported that Cox's assailant had shouted 'this is for Britain' and 'keep Britain independent' (Boffey and Slawson, 2016). Far from being random statements, these were slogans used by Britain First, a far-right fascist group, which claims to share most of the goals of the right-wing United Kingdom Independence Party (Britain First, n.d.). There are parallels here with how fear of UKIP's popularity was seen by many commentators as the inspiration for the Operation Vaken vans in 2013 (e.g. Merrick, 2013; Syal, 2013). As several of our research participants feared (see especially Chapters 4 and 5), use of increasingly hostile anti-migrant rhetoric in government and main-stream political debate seems to both authorise and fuel such hate-filled outpourings, verbal and physical.

When we began the research for this book we did not know the significance of Operation Vaken, of course. But we were disturbed by the vitriol of government rhetoric and an intensifying public mood of besiegement (Hage, 2016). These worries were shared by the community organisations with whom we developed and did the research. This way of doing research, collaboratively and with local community partners, developing 'working knowledges together' and 'partially shared imaginaries' (Suchman, 2012: 52), has helped us to include a variety of perspectives and stories of immigration enforcement, and to explore how 'the object of study is ultimately mobile and multiply situated' (Marcus, 1995:102). It has also challenged us to think more critically about the politics of immigration research and knowledge production. How are we contributing to the manner in which immigration is imagined and lived? What part does research play in the circulation and meanings of categories such as the 'immigrant', 'asylum seeker', 'refugee' and 'British citizen'? How might we produce an anti-racist and feminist 'situated knowledge' (Haraway, 1988) in a way that does not reinscribe our research participants into dominant, dehumanising discourses (see Bhavnani, 1993)?

In this chapter we will:

1   contextualise the immigration regimes and debates within which our study took place
2   describe and discuss the Go Home van and related government communications in relation to broader immigration regimes and practices
3   summarise briefly our key findings from the research, which will be developed and elaborated on throughout the book
4   outline the approach that we took in the project as activist researchers
5   provide an overview of what is in the book.

The problem of immigration

> Look at all these borders, foaming at the mouth with bodies broken and desperate.
>
> (Warsan Shire, 2011: 25)

Discussions of immigration and immigration control, securitisation and illegality have become more voluble throughout the research and writing for this book. According to the United Nations Population Fund, in 2015, 244 million people, or 3.3 per cent of the world's population, lived outside their country of origin, with increasing numbers of people being forcibly displaced as a result of conflict, violence and human rights violations (UNPF, 2016). As we worked on this manuscript in April 2016, harrowing scenes of what has become known as the Mediterranean 'refugee' or 'migrant crisis' played out in the media almost daily, as more people fleeing war, violence and poverty in Africa and the Middle East tried to find safety in Europe. Sometimes, these lives have faded from our screens and pages as another spectacle has caught journalistic and public attention, but these dangerous journeys and the trauma and deaths, 'bodies broken and desperate', that they entail continue. So far (June 2016), there have been 215,380 'arrivals' to the EU by sea in 2016; 2,868 people were reported as dead or missing on their journey to the EU in the first half of 2016 (UNHCR, 2016a). Others lost at sea go unreported. Of the nearly five million Syrians registered by the UN High Commissioner for Refugees, just over 50 per cent were women (UNHCR, 2016b). This new era of migration, which includes more women and children, is characterised for the most vulnerable by 'necropolitics'. This term was coined by the African philosopher Achille Mbembe (2003) to describe 'death worlds', where 'vast populations are subjected to conditions of life conferring upon them the status of living dead' (p. 40).

The growth of harsh new border regimes or what activist Harsha Walia (2013) calls 'border imperialism' has been a midwife to the birthing of these death worlds in Europe, not only in the Mediterranean but in planes, lorries and detention camps and centres across the continent. There are three simultaneous, imbricated developments in contemporary border regimes: the deterritorialisation of state sovereignty; a fortification of land-based borders; and the domestication of borders (Rigo, 2005; Walters, 2006; Vaughan-Williams, 2010).

The first is characterised by an outsourcing of border control, especially by those in northern Europe to more southerly nations, as increasing numbers of migrants have been heading to Europe's southern shores as part of a longer journey to destinations such as Germany, Sweden, France and Britain. Increasingly, richer countries – potential places of sanctuary – require asylum applications to be made from outside their territory (Hyndman and Mountz, 2008). This requirement extends border and migrant management into third countries, as the EU has done at different times with Turkey and Morocco (Wolff, 2008).

Alongside this deterritorialisation, the fortification of state borders can be seen in more aggressive forms of border surveillance and policing, including the building of razor-wire fences, new makeshift detention camps, and the re-establishing of border posts. The latter erodes the Schengen system of open internal borders that has been key to European integration for over two decades.

In a seemingly contradictory but actually complementary move, borders have also come 'home', entering into domestic spaces, as citizens are increasingly required to check the visa status of those they live with, work with, and serve. The UK Immigration Act 2014 brought in rules requiring private landlords to satisfy themselves that a tenant's immigration status is in order, or risk penalties. Since the Asylum and Immigration Act of 1996, employers have been obliged to check that employees meet immigration rules, or face large fines; and the Immigration Act 2016 means that banks will have to check the immigration status of people opening accounts.

Each of these developments requires increased surveillance, documentation and justification for the most basic of everyday transactions. They also make ordinary people – who are unqualified to understand often complex legal immigration documents – liable for the maintenance of border control *inside* a territory. Domesticated bordering increases suspicion and fear of the (potentially irregular) migrant and carries these into everyday personal interactions: if an irregular migrant can trick a landlord or bank clerk or human resources officer turned border guard, these proxy border guards could themselves be punished.

These changes in law and practice are heavily entwined with public feeling and discourse, as our research into performative politics demonstrates throughout the book. As we write, the last twelve months alone have seen huge shifts in what is being said in public and in local debates about migration. Throughout 2015, the press regularly carried sensationalist stories and images of people arriving in, or crossing, Europe to seek refuge. As the Lebanese-Australian anthropologist Ghassan Hage has observed, 'Hardly any newspaper – whether antagonistic to asylum seekers, such as the Australian *Daily Telegraph* (September 9, 2015), or sympathetic to their plight, such as the *Los Angeles Times* (August 6, 2015) – failed, at least occasionally, to refer to refugees in terms of "flows," "flood," and "waves"' (2016: 39). The then British Prime Minister, David Cameron, talked of 'a swarm of people coming across the Mediterranean, seeking a better life, wanting to come to Britain' (BBC, 2015). Others went further: 'these migrants are like cockroaches ... they are built to survive a nuclear bomb' wrote a *Sun* journalist (Hopkins, 2015). The potency of such visceral signifiers is that they work to reshape both the object of disgust (the migrant, or those suspected of being migrants) and the person who feels disgust. The circulation and accruing of emotions in this way is what the feminist cultural theorist Sara Ahmed (2004), drawing on the ideas of Karl Marx, calls an 'affective economy'. For

Ahmed, emotions are understood as a form of capital. They are full of value.

But emotions, for all of their power, can change. A palpable, if perhaps temporary shift, in public and political orientations towards refugees in Britain, took place on Wednesday 2 September 2015. After weeks and months of media coverage of arrivals of people by boat into Europe, a single image seemed to change the register of debate: the photograph of the dead body of three-year-old Syrian Alan Kurdi, washed up on the shores of a Turkish beach. Alan had drowned with his brother, Galip, who was five, and their mother Rehanna, when their boat sank as they tried to reach the Greek island of Kos from Bodrum in Turkey. They had previously applied (unsuccessfully) for asylum in Canada. The image of Alan elicited huge international public and political concern, perhaps because, as the writer Avan Judd Stallard (2016: n.p.) believes, Alan looked so much like a typically middle-class Western boy with 'his shirt bright red, his long shorts deep blue, his skin perfect vanilla. With arms by his side and palms facing the sky, it looked as if he had fallen and could not get up.' Whatever it was about the image that moved people, more and more individuals across Europe began to offer support to displaced people in large and small ways: signing online petitions, sending money, visiting refugee camps, joining protests and offering shelter in their own homes (Jones, 2015).

In the UK, this shift in public sympathies led to the government promising that it would take more refugees (having previously refused to participate in any international plan). It was announced that the UK would take twenty thousand Syrian refugees – coming through the UN resettlement programme – over five years. Rather than relocating people who were already in Europe, Britain would be resettling those from refugee camps in the region. In effect a territorial border and the 'problem' of refugees was moved from Europe to Syria, and a moral border was drawn around Syrians as legitimate (see Holmes and Castañeda, 2016) and deserving refugees (see also Chapter 5). The number (twenty thousand) was seen to be large, but once spread across five years, and across regions of the UK, meant that few families would arrive in any one area.[2] Thus the move enabled national

---

[2] A survey published in early July 2016 found that a third of UK councils have refused to take in Syrian refugees because they lack the financial resources to support them. See www.ibtimes.co.uk/one-third-councils-refuse-house-syrian-refugees-due-high-accommodation-costs-1569340 [last accessed 8 July 2016].

government to assuage growing public pressure for the UK to do something to help refugees, while effectively limiting its (conditional) hospitality.

The identification of Syrian refugees specifically as deserving of help (and the downgrading of the lives of others seeking refuge from elsewhere) changed again on 13 November, as media reported that a Syrian passport had been found near the body of one of the suspected terrorist attackers in Paris. In the attack 130 people had been murdered (the Islamic State of Iraq and the Levant 'ISIL' later claimed responsibility for the violence). Three days afterwards, the then Home Secretary, Theresa May, gave a speech associating immigrants with terrorists, superimposing an announcement of 'targeted security checks' on to a promise of more stringent control at both national and European borders. The point here is that the ways in which immigration and immigration enforcement emerge as a problem are continually evolving. This includes not only how categories of 'them' and 'us' are open to revision but also how these categories can be mediated by moments of, and movements between, indifference, welcome, compassion and conviviality (see Brah, 2012/1999; Jones and Jackson, 2014).

In the months following the Paris attacks, Britain's political debate increasingly focused on campaigns about whether to 'leave' or 'remain' in the European Union, with both sides focused on immigration. The Leave campaigners emphasised a promise to 'control immigration' and the Remain campaign appeared to offer something similar, though slightly less stridently. Over months, confusion abounded over what exactly was meant by immigration control. Would EU citizens in the UK have their residency rights removed? Would Britons have their residency rights, and freedom of movement, in other EU countries revoked in return? What would it mean, if anything, for non-EU citizens wanting to live in Britain? No specific details were given, except that immigration would be more 'in control' following the referendum, whatever the result. And it was promised that consequently, there would be an easing of the problems of limited jobs, housing and disinvestment in the NHS. These promises came from government ministers campaigning on both sides, and senior politicians and public figures.

In this atmosphere, on Thursday 16 June, exactly one week before the referendum vote, the then UKIP Leader and prominent Vote Leave campaigner Nigel Farage launched a poster with the words 'Breaking Point: The EU has failed us all. We must break free of the EU and take back control of our borders'. The words appeared above an image of a crowded queue of Syrian refugees at the Slovenian border. Immediate parallels were drawn with similar images used in German Nazi propaganda (Lister, 2016). A few hours after the poster was unveiled, the Labour MP and pro-migrant Remain campaigner Jo Cox was murdered outside her constituency office by a man whom witnesses said they heard shouting far-right nationalist slogans.

Farage dismissed any connection between the temperature of the debate on migration and the assassination of Jo Cox, stating: 'The Remain camp are using these awful circumstances to try to say that the motives of one deranged, dangerous individual are similar to half the country, or perhaps more, who believe we should leave the EU' (quoted in Smith, 2016: n.p.). This was the same man who, a month earlier, had said: 'It's legitimate to say that if people feel they've lost control completely, and we have lost control of our borders completely as members of the EU, and if people feel voting doesn't change anything, then violence is the next step' (quoted in Simons, 2016: n.p.).

Farage's latter prediction seems to be materialising. His Leave campaign won the referendum, but, as we completed this book in the days following that result, the vote seemed to have changed both everything and nothing. Everything, as there was apparently no plan about how to proceed, no political leadership within the government (following the Prime Minister's resignation and before Theresa May's appointment as his replacement), or opposition (as Labour MPs attempted to remove their leader). There are dramatic economic fluctuations and uncertainty, with the renewed possibility of Scottish independence since Scotland voted strongly to remain in the EU, and increasing political fracturing between the almost equally divided voters across the country.

And nothing, because, in the days following the result, all key Leave campaigners insisted that they had never promised to reduce immigration, or to invest money they claimed would be saved from EU contributions into the NHS. In the days immediately after the referendum it emerged that there was no plan of how to begin negotiations or renegotiate the UK's relationship to the EU, or what this might mean in practice. And yet again everything, as violence towards EU migrants and racially minoritised people appears to have been reinvigorated. 'Go home' racist catcalls and graffiti have been reported in unusual numbers, and, as it becomes clear that 'migrants' (or those assumed to be) are not going anywhere, the anger and xenophobia that have been stoked are expected to become more intense. There is a certain painful relentlessness to waking up every morning to more reports of racist abuse and violence. Our pained disbelief and depressed sighs carry the 'worrying exhale of an ache', as the poet Claudia Rankine (2014: 60) has written of the impact of living with the ongoingness of racism.

'It's all about immigration'

> I have been unprotected. I have been naked and exposed. I have been clothed and armoured. I know what I carry in my suitcase. I carry my history. I carry my family. Over my saris, I wear my sisters.
> (Shailja Patel, 2010: 41)

What has been clear at this time is how toxic and capacious the signifiers 'migrant' and 'migration' have become. People moving across state borders to settle in a new place do so for many reasons, with various citizenship and visa statuses (or their lack), with different economic and social resources, and different ethnicities and religions. The 'problem' of migration is at some points characterised simply by those who break the rules – as with the Go Home van and the question 'In the UK illegally?' This identification can slip into the association of asylum seekers as 'rule breakers', even though under the Geneva Convention it cannot be illegal to seek asylum (until that claim is accepted or rejected). There is also the slippage between seeing certain groups of migrants such as migrant workers, or 'economic migrants' as a problem, though often in the same breath there's an appeal to visa systems that might prioritise 'skilled workers' or concerns are voiced about how immigration control can damage British industries, such as the seasonal work of fruit picking. As we saw in the shifts in mood toward Syrian refugees and a later entanglement with fears of terrorism, we now also see anti-immigration rhetoric blurring with Islamophobia: 'It's all about immigration. Right, it's not about trade or Europe or anything like that, it's all about immigration. It's to stop the Muslims from coming into this country. Simple as that'. So said a 'man in the street' interviewed by a Channel 4 journalist the day the EU referendum result was announced (Jenkins, 2016).

As we write in this politically volatile context, we ask: what does it mean to live in this time of an obsession with borders and where 'taking back control' holds such a political and psychological appeal? How do different groups of people – migrants and refugees, policymakers, British citizens and pro-migrant activists – understand and narrate the 'problem' of immigration and its control? How might we make a problem out of the problem of immigration?

Operation Vaken

It is with these questions in mind that we tell the story of our Mapping Immigration Controversy project. The study, funded by the Economic and Social Research Council, investigated Operation Vaken that took place between 22 July and 22 August 2013. The short-lived, two-week Home Office campaign in England, Scotland and Wales included the Go Home vans discussed earlier. There was also a separate pilot scheme where 'Ask about going home' posters were put up in detention centres in Glasgow and Hounslow (see Chapter 4 for more detail).

Vaken is most often associated with the two Go Home vans that were driven through six of the most ethnically diverse London boroughs (Hounslow, Barking and Dagenham, Ealing, Barnet, Brent and Redbridge). The full message carried by the vans (see Figure 1) read: 'In the UK illegally? GO HOME OR FACE ARREST. Text HOME to 78070 for free advice, and help with travel documents. We can help you return home voluntarily without fear of arrest or detention.' Along with these words was a close-up of a border guard's uniform and handcuffs, a telephone number to call, and the claim: '106 ARRESTS LAST WEEK IN YOUR AREA'. At the time of the piloting of Vaken, the Home Office issued press releases and Twitter updates, reporting on arrests of 'immigration offenders'. The official Home Office Twitter account shared images of immigration raids, showing people being put into the back of secure vans. The tweets read, 'There will be no hiding place for illegal immigrants with the new #immigration-bill'. Another hashtag was #immigrationoffender.

Not surprisingly it was the visual drama of the vans that attracted much press coverage and commentary from politicians, civil society organisations and the public. As well as eliciting anger, the vans became objects of 'play', a source of satire and ridicule in the 'reverberation' (Kuntsman, 2012) of feelings between online and offline worlds. The Liberal Democrat Cabinet Minister Vince Cable, speaking on the BBC, said that the campaign was 'stupid and offensive', adding, 'It is designed, apparently, to sort of create a sense of fear [in the] British population that we have a vast problem with illegal immigration' (Huff Post Politics, UK, 2013, n.p.). Images of the vans circulated quickly on social media, along with the hashtag #racistvan, directly connecting the language used with the history of the words 'go home' as racist abuse used in the streets and by far-right political groups such as the National Front in the 1970s.

In response to criticisms of Vaken, the then Minister for Immigration, Mark Harper, wrote an article in the tabloid newspaper the *Daily Mail* on 29 July 2013, saying that he had been 'astonished' by the reactions of the 'Left and pro-immigration industry' that had denounced Vaken as racist. 'Let me clear this up once and for all', Harper wrote, 'it is not racist to ask people who are here illegally to leave Britain. It is merely telling them to comply with the law. Our campaign targets illegal immigrants without any discrimination at all between them. By no stretch of the rational imagination can it be described as "racist" ' (Harper, 2013a: n.p.). This rhetorical move to separate out racism from immigration control was not new. As the cultural theorist Paul Gilroy (2012) has observed, it was during New Labour's administrations, between 1997 and 2010, that 'the bogus proposition that race and immigration could be easily untangled in Britain's political culture held sway' (p. 380). This proposition holds that to be anti-migrant or anti-immigration is not the same as being racist. It was a rhetoric that did not go unchallenged.

On 2 August 2013, Doreen Lawrence (an anti-racist campaigner and Labour peer) added her voice to surfacing claims that Vaken's immigration enforcement checks at railway and Tube stations were based on racial profiling, targeting racially minoritised commuters. 'I'm sure there's illegal immigrants from all countries, but why would you focus that on people of colour, and I think racial profiling is coming into it', she said (Malik and Batty, 2013). Civil society organisations were also taking action to highlight Vaken's racist tropes and the kindling of racism and suspicion within local communities. Three days before Harper's article on 26 July, the Refugee and Migrant Forum of Essex and London (RAMFEL) (one of our community partners in the research for this book) held 'an emergency tension-monitoring' meeting with Home Office officials. On 31 July, RAMFEL announced that it had written to the Department to inform it of legal action to declare Vaken unlawful. In RAMFEL's words:

> Two service users from RAMFEL, supported by Deighton Pierce Glynn launched a legal challenge against the Home Office based on the fact that there had been no consultation done with anyone (community organisations, and local councils and borough police) and that the Home Office had failied [*sic*] to pay due regard to equality and cohesion issues. Further legal action was precluded by the fact that the Operation Vaken was a pilot.
>
> (RAMFEL, n.d.)

In a written statement to Parliament in October 2013, Mark Harper gave this retrospective rationale for Vaken:

> It is better for both the UK taxpayer and offenders themselves if offenders leave the country voluntarily rather than in an enforced manner. Immigration Compliance and Enforcement teams are therefore working to identify how they can promote the visibility of enforcement operations to drive compliance and encourage more immigration offenders to leave the UK voluntarily.
>
> (Harper, 2013b: n.p.)

In short then, Vaken was presented as being for the benefit not only of immigration offenders but also of the UK taxpayer. The campaign was subsequently condemned by the Advertising Standards Authority for using inaccurate information (the '106 arrests in your area' claim was inaccurate; see ASA, 2013). On 21 October, the Home Secretary announced that Vaken would be scrapped. Yet this drive to communications campaigns by national government, ostensibly targeted at immigration offenders but with an audience of the law-abiding and taxpaying public in mind, continued. This extended to similar measures over the following years, including an increased visibility of marked Home Office Enforcement vans on raids around the UK; signs in hospital waiting rooms declaring 'The NHS is not free for everyone' to highlight limited access to 'universal' healthcare for some migrants (see Figure 2); press releases on immigration enforcement activities; and ride-alongs for local and national journalists on immigration raids.

In fact, the spectacle-making of British immigration enforcement was not something that began in 2013. There was a clear turning point in the UK government approach to migration policy in around 2006, under a Labour government. A policy consensus in Whitehall and Westminster reached the conclusion that, while immigration had been a long-standing concern in public opinion polls (see Blinder, 2015), any previous attempts to define migration as good for the UK, particularly in economic and cultural terms, appeared to have no effect in increasing positive pro-immigration views and feelings. Instead, hostility to new immigration seems to have been taken as a given, and government resources invested in demonstrating a visibly tough approach to controlling borders and movement. In 2006, under the then Home Secretary John Reid, the visibility of UK Border Control at ports was increased, with new uniforms and signage, and politicians and journalists accompanying enforcement officers on photogenic immigration raids.

These changes in immigration enforcement are related to the increasing militarisation of policing and control in the UK that has taken place over decades. The changes happened incrementally and through the targeting of particular demonised groups, such as striking miners or rioting black youth, bringing tactics previously deployed in Northern Ireland to the British mainland.

Through the 1970s and 1980s to the present day, the physical appearance and weaponry employed shifted from a police force that did not differentiate between the appearance and uniform of the 'bobby on the beat' and officers deployed in urban disturbances, to become actively intimidating. After the Brixton disturbances in the summer of 1981, and while Lord Scarman was still compiling his report into the events, the results of a review of 'protective clothing and equipment' announced that in future the police would have special riot gear: overalls, 'NATO' helmets, special shields (short and long), special riot batons (much longer and thicker than usual), 'protective' screens for transits, and CS gas and plastic bullets (Bunyan, 1985: 301). The language throughout was militaristic, speaking of gaining and holding ground, seeking 'strategic' advantage and inducing fear (Bunyan, 1985: 302).

The 2006 introduction of newly branded staff and vehicles to undertake immigration enforcement, including the extension of immigration raids with the accompanying militarised uniforms and dogs, could be regarded as another development of this militarised approach to public order. Just as the introduction of military-derived equipment for police officers was deployed to induce fear among particular targeted groups, shows of force in the name of immigration enforcement might also be regarded as a tactical performance of power.

During the period of escalating militarisation of policing through the 1970s and 1980s, this uneven performance of violent intent was communicated as a confirmation that there were indeed enemies within. In this framework the performance of power has two distinct audiences – those who are the immediate target of coercive power and those who must be persuaded that the state is exerting its powers against dangerous 'others'.

As we will go on to explain (see Chapter 2), we understand Vaken as part of this developing 'performative politics' (Rai, 2015) of immigration control, in which emotions are recruited and played upon. Margaret Wetherell's (2012) notion of 'affective practice' as including situated discourses, practices and bodily states, has helped us to think through and apply the ideas of the political theorist Shirin Rai (2015) on political performance to our empirical research (discussed further in Chapter 2). Rai describes political performance as 'Those performances that seek to communicate to an audience meaning-making related to state institutions, policies and discourses' (2015: 1179). However, the extent to which such communication is successful in achieving its intended effects is always locally contingent and unstable (see also Austin, 1975/1962).

The hate speech of a politician or a journalist, for instance, can overlap with what is said in a café or in a focus group interview, but the power and consequences of each of these speech acts are not the same. Because our project included various levels of research that moved between texts and policy discourses, such as the post-hoc rationale for Vaken given by Mark Harper, to talk-in-interaction in social media, to observation and one-to-one interviews and focus groups in different localities, we have been able to decipher some of the continuities as well as what Wetherell calls the 'different compositional logic' (2012: 159) of the affective practices surrounding Vaken. As we show in Chapter 4, the localities in which elements of government communications campaigns were deployed, and the ways opposition to them was mobilised, shaped how the campaign was variously felt and responded to in different contexts.

What we found

Throughout the book, we discuss the findings of our research in detail. Our data and analysis are intertwined, and we draw on existing knowledge and theory in the social sciences to make sense of what we have found. Here, though, we summarise very briefly what our research uncovered.

1   We found **no evidence that government communications about immigration and enforcement are based on research about 'what works'** in managing immigration. The only research evidence policy-makers mentioned to us was privately commissioned research on managing public opinion about immigration, particularly among those worried that immigration is 'out of control'. Yet our research suggests the tactics used on this basis can increase fear and anxiety.

2   **Government campaigns on immigration provoked or increased anger and fear**, among irregular migrants,

regular migrants and non-migrants, including those opposed to immigration. The latter told us they thought that the government campaigns were ineffective 'theatre'.

3   For people who were the subjects of immigration campaigns (or felt under threat from them), talking about the publicity campaigns often led them to think about their own experiences of immigration enforcement and triggered feelings of fear and anxiety. **Our own research focused on communications campaigns, but participants also made direct links to, for example, images of enforcement raids and their own experiences of immigration enforcement in their homes.**

4   **Hard-hitting government publicity on immigration seemed to provoke new waves of pro-migrant activism.** Anger and outrage was translated into online and street-based activism, including by people who had not been engaged in activism before.

5   Some, but not all, activism has been migrant-led, and **we identified inequalities in who felt able to take part in political debate because of real or perceived threats to their residency status as a result.**

6   **Traditional anti-racism campaigns are finding it hard to keep up with changes in the focus of hostility and discrimination,** for example with how to engage with the status of international students and asylum seekers.

7   Our local case studies demonstrated **local variations in how government campaigns were experienced, and the activism that was produced in response.** In some places migrants and activists could build on existing infrastructures for political organising. In other places such resources did not exist or had dwindled, or energies were focused on service provision for vulnerable people in an increasingly difficult funding environment.

8   **There is not always solidarity between people being targeted by anti-immigration campaigns.** We found several instances of hostility between different groups of migrants, often based on an idea that their own group was 'deserving' of residency and status in the UK, while others were 'undeserving'.

9   The different legal statuses that migrants can have is confusing. For many people in the wider public, the distinctions between 'illegal' and 'legal', and between asylum

seeker, refugee, student, worker, resident, and sometimes between migrants and ethnic minority British-born people is difficult to understand. **Many people reported harassment for being 'illegal immigrants' when they had settled status, or were British citizens.**

10 **We heard that many people had come to the UK because of ideals often promoted as 'British values'** – such as democracy, the rule of law, individual liberty and mutual respect and tolerance for those with different faiths and beliefs. **Their experience since arrival called into doubt the existence of these values.**

Researching immigration

As well as telling the story of government immigration communication campaigns, we want to contribute to thinking and discussions about the role of critical migration research and the relationships between activism and research (see also Casas-Cortes et al., 2014; Walia, 2013). There is a 'civic task' at stake in how we make use of our sociological imaginations in such endeavours, the sociologist Alberto Toscano argues, which 'is not to create pacifying knowledge, but to sharpen and concretise what would otherwise be a vague and powerless anxiety, while at the same time providing a realistic estimate of the powers necessary to alter, however minimally, the course of history' (2012: 68). The term 'militant investigation' (Casas-Cortes et al., 2014) has been used more recently to refer to new ways of thinking about and doing migration research, although research propelled by a 'civic task' has a long history in early British research on migration and race, such as the studies *Race, Community and Conflict* by John Rex and Robert Moore (1967), Elizabeth Burney's *Housing on Trial* (1967), *Racial Discrimination in England* (Daniel, 1968) and *Because They're Black* (Humphry and John, 1971).

For us, it was crucially important that we connected and extended the civic task of sociology to the structures and practices of actually doing the research. The MIC team included early career academics and more established scholars. We are predominantly women, and women of various ethnicities and migration histories. An aspiration of our research, from the very beginning, is outlined in a warning from Stuart Hall and his 'Policing the Crisis' (1978) co-authors: we tried not to fall into 'a trap of "liberal opinion" – to split analysis from action' (Hall et al., 1978: ix). As we have already mentioned, our research began in July 2013 with unfunded street surveys to capture, as quickly as we could, reactions to Vaken (details of the methods we used are in the Appendix). At the time, our primary aim was to record and provide some evidence of the impact of Vaken, and more ambitiously to intervene in and encourage public discussions of immigration enforcement.

However, on the same day that we began to foment the idea of immediate action research to counter Vaken, we were separately alerted to a call for proposals by the Urgent Research Grant scheme of the Economic and Social Research Council. It seemed to be worth a try to do something bigger and more systematic. In putting our funding proposal together, we consolidated our connections with local civil society organisations that were interested in doing some of the research with us in their local areas. Their time was costed into the proposal (see Living Research Six). The organisations helped us to shape our overall research questions and research design, to identify activists and community workers to interview in each area, recruited participants for our focus groups and invited us to local events and meetings where immigration enforcement was being discussed. They also helped us to set up feedback sessions, where we took the interim findings of our research back to open meetings in each community, and learned more from their responses, which in turn were fed into our emerging analysis.

In brief, the research methods that we used in the study consisted of:

- 13 focus groups with 67 people (including new migrants, long-settled migrants, ethnic minority and white British citizens)
- 24 one-to-one interviews with local activists
- interviews with eight national policy-makers about the intentions and thinking behind immigration enforcement campaigns
- a survey commissioned from Ipsos MORI to investigate awareness of and attitudes to immigration enforcement. Questions were placed on the Ipsos MORI Omnibus (Capibus) amongst a nationally representative quota sample of 2,424 adults (aged 15 and over). Interviews were conducted face-to-face in respondents' homes between 15 August and 9 September 2014, using Computer Assisted Personal Interviewing software. All data are weighted to the known national profile of adults aged 15+ in Great Britain.
- participation in and documentation of online debates on Twitter about key elements of Vaken and related campaigns, and reactions to them

- presenting and discussing interim findings with the communities and organisations with whom we had done the initial research, and including their responses in the findings
- fieldnotes of interviews and ethnographic observation that we used to help us develop more multisensory and reflexive insights.

The approach we took in the project comes closest to the ethos of 'live sociology', which is the term coined by sociologist Les Back (2007; 2012) for a sociology that is civic, dialogic and multisensory (see also Back and Puwar, 2012). Live sociology for Back is 'histori-cally situated, reflective, contestable, uncomfortable, partisan and fraught' (2007: 22), with an 'intellectual architecture' attentive to the 'scope and scale of global social processes' (2012: 20). One way in which we tried to be receptive to matters of 'scope and scale' in the statecraft of immigration communications was to use a combination of qualitative and quantitative methods. By working across methods and sites of research, including the digital, we were able to connect the more nuanced and intimate responses that we elicited through our face-to-face interviews and observations to larger, more distanced and distributed affective patterns. Our survey not only focused attention on immigration enforcement, we were also able to contextualise some of our questions with regard to racism (see Chapter 2). A vital aspect of our 'live sociology' is that it has been collaborative throughout (see Living Research Six). This included producing research in partner-ship with those outside the academy, communicating our thoughts and engagement with immigration politics as they unfolded in real time through blog posts and Twitter. And, not least, the imagining, writing, editing and redrafting of this book have been a collective effort.

About this book

Throughout the book, we draw upon ideas and theories from cultural studies, economics, politics, media and communications and sociol-ogy to develop an account of contemporary British immigration enforcement politics. There are six substantive chapters, which begin by contextualising Vaken with regard to the performative politics of immigration control (Chapter 2) and post-liberal governmentality (Chapter 3). Chapters 4 and 5 provide a more close-up analysis of our empirical research, situating the research within space and place (Chapter 4) and critically examining narratives of the 'deserving' and 'undeserving' migrant, and ways these characterisations have been resisted (Chapter 5). Chapter 6, our concluding chapter, brings together the key themes from our research and raises questions about the developing politics of immigration control at the critical and fast-changing moment in which we complete this book.

The chapters are separated by short interludes that we have titled 'Living Research'. These are reflective pieces, breathing and thinking spaces that offer our thoughts and experiences of doing the research. They cover why we did the research (Living Research One); the methodological challenges of researching emotionally charged topics (Two); the politics of migration research and the media (Three); ethics (Four); how social media and social research allowed us to channel and also connect our anger at Vaken with others (Five); and how the collaborative aspects of the research worked (and didn't work) in practice (Six). The Living Research sections are intended to incite thinking and dialogue about these issues of the politics and practice, as well as the findings, of research. For this reason we also include some questions for the reader to reflect on, whether in a group or independently.

Our understanding of Vaken draws on the framework of perfor-mance politics proposed by the political scientist Shirin Rai (2015). In Chapter 2 we describe and use Rai's work to make sense of the deployment of theatricalised violence by the British state in which performances of state power are directed at many audiences and serve to segment the population. Drawing on our research we suggest that, despite attempts to address a diversity of audiences, commu-nications and performances of immigration policing appear to be met with indifference or anxiety. They can also be reinterpreted through a popular cynicism that is influenced by a broader culture of anti-politics. Chapter 2 explores the impact of such scepticism on the politics of migration, and asks whether there are possibilities for a politics based on mutuality.

In Chapter 3 we consider how the politicisation of British immigra-tion policy tests the limits of 'liberal governmentality' (Rose and Miller, 1992). Typically, this form of government is understood in terms of splitting questions of 'politics' from those of 'expertise', employing statistics, professions, economics, audits and so on, to insulate certain issues as matters of 'fact' or 'efficiency'. 'Blackboxing' political questions through the use of statistics (and utilitarian assump-tions), we suggest, is a way of preventing them from turning into controversies which invite public deliberation. Immigration is an exception that evades this bracketing. More emotional, story-based impressions of immigration, often cultivated by the media, appear hard to dislodge through statistical data. Under these circumstances, policy-makers have engaged in different types of knowledge acquisition and production, focusing on the affective, emotional and symbolic dimensions of immigration. This involves unwieldy combinations of pre-liberal sovereign performances (parading state violence) with postliberal attempts to manipulate affect (nudging and social marketing). Here, by engaging with policy-makers' accounts of the negotiations they make in this context, we explore the strains that immigration control places on liberal governmentality, with its desire to separate technical decisions from politics, and the challenge posed by postliberal approaches which emphasise morality and distinctions between deserving and undeserving subjects.

Having contextualised the Go Home van and other government anti-immigration communications as part of a performative politics that challenges liberal governmentality, we move on to situate these developments by considering the part played by spaces and places – from the street to the digital realm – in the implementation and reception of, and resistance to, anti-immigration campaigns (Chapter 4). For us, such interventions are closely tied to the increasingly domestic nature of immigration control and as they are enacted in particular spaces, with different local histories of migration and activism, they have had unintended consequences. These include increased fear, feelings of not belonging and acts of resistance. For instance, we discuss how opposition to Go Home posters in Glasgow fed into debates about Scottish Independence and how the Go Home vans' appearance in West London played into divisive discourses of respectability among more established migrants and British citizens. We argue that it is vital to consider specific sites of immigration intervention and resistance (e.g. the hospital waiting room, Twitter) and how local and urban contexts shape and are shaped by reaction and resistance when examining the impact of anti-immigration campaigns.

The distinctions between 'deserving' and 'undeserving' migrants (and citizens), that are made by local people, including those from racially minoritised communities and recent immigrants, are the subject of Chapter 5. Our research has found a certain complicity with anti-immigrant messages and, as diverse local communities compete over limited resources, the exacerbation of latent tensions. In making sense of these findings, we use Bridget Anderson's exploration of 'communities of value' (2013), Imogen Tyler's theorisation of social abjection (2013) and Beverley Skeggs' examination of the politics of respectability in relation to gender and class (1997; 2014). In an intersectional analysis we look at the fracturing of the connections between 'race' and immigration and discuss the role of socially conservative codes of respectability in internalising disgust towards particular social groups – sex workers, the destitute and people using alcohol and drugs (some of who are assumed to have irregular immigration status).

Our own

The proliferation of domestic immigration enforcement, the seemingly more mundane and shadowy 'other' of international border control and necropolitics, has uneven and unexpected effects. Immigration is itself an internally differentiated experience of inclusion and exclusion (Erel, 2010) and of changing identifications (La Barbera, 2013).

We know that the damage inflicted by enforcement campaigns can be slow-paced and dispersed across lives. It is difficult to quantify and capture. Operation Vaken was terrifying for some people. For others, it signalled the authorising and normalisation of the public expression of hostility towards immigration and migrants. 'It is now acceptable to come out and say I am anti-immigration' one person told us in a focus group interview.

If government communications on immigration lend a certain respectability to anti-migrant feelings and racism, we should not forget that it can also galvanise opposition and dissent, both serious and playful. The government's own evaluation of the Operation Vaken makes for interesting reading (Home Office, 2013). Of the 1,561 text messages received by the Home Office, 1,034 were hoax messages, taking up 17 hours of staff time. At the time of writing, the YouTube film of one of our research partners, Southall Black Sisters, disrupting a Vaken immigration raid has been viewed over 39,000 times,[3] suggesting an impact much wider than the original spontaneous event (discussed further in Living Research One and Five and Chapter 4).

There are plenty more examples of dissent from the politics of suspicion and hatred, signifying what the political scholar Vicki Squire (2011) thinks of as 'mobile solidarities' – collective engagements and small acts of hospitality that cut across social hierarchies and divisions. We also take heart from the work of the feminist and postcolonial theorist Avtar Brah, whose doctoral research (1979) in three schools in Southall in the 1970s, sought to better understand the interrelations between race, ethnicity and class in this fast-changing West London community. Brah's research picked up on similar themes to ours in

---

[3] www.youtube.com/watch?v=pQ0_TFBVots [last accessed 27 June 2016].

the interplay between xenophobia and racism, the feelings of resentment, fear and antipathy to the arrival of migrants from India and the Caribbean. At the same time Brah (2012/1999: 20–1) identified complicated and ambivalent affinities across lines of class, gender and ethnicity, expressed most beautifully in the South Asian creole language of Urdu. Urdu recognises dynamic movements between the positions of 'ajnabi' ('a stranger; a newcomer whom one does not yet know but who holds the promise of friendship, love, intimacy'), 'ghair' (where difference 'walks the tightrope between insider/outsider') and 'apna' ('one of our own').

As borders continue to mobilise and insinuate themselves across and within our everyday lives, our hope is that so will resistance and a more unconditional hospitality to migrants, who might yet cross the most significant frontier, moving across the boundary of the ajnabi into the space of the apne (plural) – our own.

References

Agerholm, H. (2016) 'Brexit: Wave of racial abuse and hate crime reported after EU referendum', *The Independent*, 26 June, www.independent. co.uk/news/uk/home-news/brexit-eu-referendum-racial-racism-abuse-hate-crime-reported-latest-leave-immigration-a7104191. html [last accessed 26 June 2016].

Ahmed, S. (2004) *The Cultural Politics of Emotion*, New York: Routledge.

Anderson, B. (2013) *Us and Them? The Dangerous Politics of Immigration Control*, Oxford: Oxford University Press.

ASA (2013) *ASA Ruling on Home Office*, 9 October, www.asa.org.uk/ Rulings/Adjudications/2013/10/Home-Office/SHP_ADJ _237331.aspx#.V3BnWegrLIU [last accessed 26 June 2016].

Austin, J.L. (1975/1962) *How to Do Things with Words*, 2nd ed., Oxford: Oxford University Press.

Back, L. (2007) *The Art of Listening*, Oxford: Berg.

Back, L. (2012) 'Live sociology: social research and its futures', *The Sociological Review*, 60 (S1): 18–39.

Back, L. and Puwar, N. (2012) 'A manifesto for live methods: provocations and capacities', *The Sociological Review*, 60 (S1): 6–17.

BBC (2015) 'David Cameron criticised over migrant "swarm" language', *BBC News*, 30 July, www.bbc.co.uk/news/uk-politics-33716501 [last accessed 30 April 2016].

BBC News (2016) 'Anti-Polish cards in Huntingdon after EU referendum', *BBC News*, 26 June, www.bbc.co.uk/news/uk-england-cambridgeshire-36633388?SThisFB [last accessed 26 June 2016].

Berger, J. and Mohr, J. (1975/2010) *A Seventh Man*, London: Verso.

Bhavnani, K.-K. (1993) 'Tracing the contours of feminist research and feminist objectivity', *Women's Studies International Forum*, 6 (2): 95–104.

Blinder, S. (2015) *UK Public Opinion toward Immigration: Overall Attitudes and Level of Concern*, Migration Observatory: University of Oxford, www.migrationobservatory.ox.ac.uk/briefings/uk-public-opinion-toward-immigration-overall-attitudes-and-level-concern [last accessed 30 April 2016].

Boffey, D. and Slawson, N. (2016) 'Jo Cox murder accused gives name as "death to traitors, freedom for Britain" ', *The Guardian*, 18 June, www.theguardian.com/uk-news/2016/jun/18/jo-cox-murder-suspect-thomas-mair-told-police-he-was-political-activist [last accessed 26 June 2016].

Brah, A. (1979) *Inter-Generational and Inter-Ethnic Perceptions: A Comparative Study of English and Asian Adolescents and Their Parents in Southall*, PhD thesis: University of Bristol.

Brah, A. (2012/1999) 'The *Scent of Memory*: strangers, our own, and others', *Feminist Review*, 100: 27–38.

Britain First (n.d.) 'Where does Britain First and UKIP differ? Answer: Islam', www.britainfirst.org/where-does-britain-first-and-ukip-differ-answer-islam/ [last accessed 26 June 2016].

Bunyan, T. (1985) 'From Saltley to Orgreave via Brixton', *Journal of Law and Society*, 12 (3): 293–303.

Burney, E. (1967) *Housing on Trial*, Oxford: Oxford University Press.

Casas-Cortes, M., Cobarrubias, S., De Genova, N., Garelli, G., Grappi, G., Heller, C., Hess, S., Kasparek, B., Mezzadra, S., Neilson, B., Peano, I., Pezzani, L., Pickles, J., Rahola, F., Riedner, L., Scheel, S. and Tazzioli, M. (2014) 'New keywords: migration and borders', *Cultural Studies*, 29 (1): 1–33.

Daniel, W.W. (1968) *Racial Discrimination in England*, Harmondsworth: Penguin Books.

Erel, U. (2010) 'Migrating cultural capital: Bourdieu in Migration Studies', *Sociology*, 44 (4): 642–60.

Gilroy, P. (2012) ' "My Britain is fuck all" zombie multiculturalism and the race politics of citizenship', *Identities: Global Studies in Culture and Power*, 19 (4): 380–97.

Gunaratnam, Y. and Patel, P. (2015) 'The hypocrisy of immigration politics: Compassion at a distance', 29 April, www.newleftproject.org/index.php/site/article_comments/the_hypocrisy_of_immigration_politics_compassion_at_a_distance [last accessed 26 June 2016].

Hage, G. (2016) 'Etat de sège: A dying domesticating colonialism?', *American Ethnologist*, 43 (1): 38–49.

Hall, S., Critcher, C., Jefferson, T., Clarke, J. and Roberts, B. (1978) *Policing the Crisis: Mugging, the State, and Law and Order*, Basingstoke: Macmillan Education.

Haraway, D. (1988) 'Situated knowledges: the science question in feminism and the privilege of partial perspective', *Feminist Studies*, 14 (3): 575–99.

Harper, M. (2013a) 'Racism? It is not racist to ask people who are here illegally to leave Britain', *The Daily Mail*, 29 July, www.dailymail.co.uk/news/article-2381051/MARK-HARPER-Racism-It-racist-ask-people-illegally-leave-Britain.html#ixzz3pUKlqpJ3 [last accessed 30 April 2016].

Harper, M. (2013b) 'Written statement to Parliament', *Immigration Enforcement: Operation Vaken*, 13 October, www.gov.uk/government/speeches/immigration-enforcement-operation-vaken [last accessed 30 April 2016].

Holmes, S. and Castañeda, H. (2016) 'Representing the "European refugee crisis" in Germany and beyond: Deservingness and difference, life and death', *American Ethnologist*, 43 (1): 12–24, http://onlinelibrary.wiley.com/doi/10.1111/amet.12259/full [last accessed 30 April 2016].

Home Office (2013) *Operation Vaken: Evaluation Report*, 31 October, www.gov.uk/government/publications/operation-vaken-evaluation-report [last accessed 12 May 2016].

Hopkins, K. (2015) 'Rescue Boats? I'd use gunships to stop migrants', *The Sun*, 17 April, www.thesun.co.uk/sol/homepage/suncolumnists/katiehopkins/6414865/Katie-Hopkins-I-would-use-gunships-to-stop-migrants.html?CMP=spklr-_-Editorial-_-TWITTER-_-TheSunNewspaper-_-20150417-_-Opinion/Columnists-_-169521585 [last accessed 30 April 2016].

Huff Post Politics UK (2013) 'Vince Cable: immigration crackdown and #RacistVan is "stupid and offensive" ', *The Huffington Post UK*, 28 July, www.huffingtonpost.co.uk/2013/07/28/cable-immigration_n_3666286.html?utm_hp_ref=uk [last accessed 30 April 2016].

Humphry, D. and John, G. (1971) *Because They're Black*, London: Penguin.

Hyndman, J. and Mountz, A. (2008) 'Another brick in the wall? Neo-refoulement and the externalization of asylum by Australia and Europe', *Government and Opposition*, 43 (2): 249–69.

Jenkins, C. (2016) 'Immigration. Patriotism. Muslims. People explain why they voted #Leave', *Twitter*, 24 June, https://twitter.com/C4Ciaran/status/746415597882220544 [last accessed 26 June 2016].

Jones, H. (2015) 'Public opinion on the refugee crisis is changing fast – and for the better', *The Conversation*, 4 September, http://theconversation.com/public-opinion-on-the-refugee-crisis-is-changing-fast-and-for-the-better-47064 [last accessed 26 June 2016].

Jones, H. and Jackson, E. (eds) (2014) *Stories of Cosmopolitan Belonging: Emotion and Location*, London: Routledge/Earthscan.

Judd Stallard, A. (2016) 'The Outsiders', *Aeon*, 1 June, https://aeon.co/essays/does-evolution-explain-the-social-antipathy-to-refugees [last accessed 26 June 2016].

Kuntsman, A. (2012) 'Introduction: Affective fabrics of digital cultures', in A. Karatzogiani and A. Kuntsman (eds), *Digital Cultures and the Politics of Emotion*, Basingstoke: Palgrave Macmillan, pp. 1–17.

La Barbera, M.C. (ed.) (2013) *Identity and Migration in Europe: Multidisciplinary Perspectives*, Cham: Springer, pp. 1–13.

Lister, S. (2016) 'Nigel Farage copies Nazi propaganda tactics as he unveils "racist" poster showing Syrian refugees', *Daily Record*, 16 June, www.dailyrecord.co.uk/news/politics/nigel-farage-copies-nazi-propaganda-8209318#EPMsiqEdx5hGDXdC.97 [last accessed 27 June 2016].

Lyons, K. (2016) 'Racist incidents feared to be linked to Brexit result', *The Guardian*, 26 June, www.theguardian.com/politics/2016/jun/26/racist-incidents-feared-to-be-linked-to-brexit-result-reported-in-england-and-wales [last accessed 26 June 2016].

Malik, S. and Batty, P. (2013) 'Doreen Lawrence questions focus on non-whites in immigrant crackdown', *The Guardian*, 2 August, www.theguardian.com/uk-news/2013/aug/02/doreen-lawrence-non-whites-immigrant-crackdown [last accessed 30 April 2016].

Marcus, G. (1995) 'Ethnography in/of the world system: The Emergence of multi-sited ethnography', *Annual Review of Anthropology*, 24: 95–117.

Mbembe, A. (2003) 'Necropolitics', *Public Culture*, 15(1): 11–40.

Merrick, J. (2013) 'Nick Clegg not involved in the the "go home" campaign: how the "racist van" is a way to win votes', *The Independent*, 30 July, www.independent.co.uk/voices/comment/nick-clegg-not-involved-in-the-the-go-home-campaign-how-the-racist-van-is-a-way-to-win-votes-8738510.html [last accessed 26 June 2016].

Patel, S. (2010) *Migritude*, New York: Kaya Press.

Rai, S. (2015) 'Political performance: A framework for analysing democratic politics', *Political Studies*, 63 (5): 1179–97.

RAMFEL (n.d.) *Campaigning and Lobbying on Immigration, Equality and Diversity Issues*, www.ramfel.org.uk/wordpress/campaigning/ [last accessed 6 May 2016].

Rankine, C. (2014) *Citizen: An American Lyric*. Minneapolis, Minnesota: Graywolf Press.

Rex, J. and Moore, R. (1967) *Race, Community and Conflict*, Oxford: Oxford University Press.

Rigo, E. (2005) 'Citizenship at Europe's borders: Some reflections on the post-colonial condition of Europe in the context of EU enlargement', *Citizenship Studies*, 9 (1): 3–22.

Rose, N. and Miller, P. (1992) 'Political power beyond the state: Problematics of government', *The British Journal of Sociology*, 43(2): 173–205.

Shire, W. (2011) *Teaching My Mother How to Give Birth*, London: Mouthmark.

Simons, N. (2016) 'Nigel Farage predicts "violence the next step" if immigration is not controlled', *HuffPost Politics*, 17 May, www.huffingtonpost.co.uk/entry/nigel-farage-predicts-violence-the-next-step-if-immigration-is-not-controlled_uk_573b8f77e4b0328a838b8c9c [last accessed 26 June 2016].

Skeggs, B. (1997) *Formations of Class and Gender: Becoming Respectable*, London: Sage.

Skeggs, B. (2014) 'Values beyond value: Is there anything beyond the logic of capital?', *British Journal of Sociology*, 65 (1): 1–20.

Smith, M. (2016) 'Nigel Farage claims "ALL of the Remain camp" are "using" Jo Cox's death for their political advantage', *Mirror*, 20 June, www.mirror.co.uk/news/uk-news/nigel-farage-claims-all-remain-8236531 [last accessed 26 June 2016].

Squire, V. (2011) 'From community cohesion to *mobile solidarities*: The city of sanctuary network and the strangers into citizenship campaign', *Political Studies*, 59 (2): 290–307.

Staufenberg, J. (2016) 'Brexit: Welsh Muslim told to "pack bags and go home" after campaigning for Remain', *The Independent*, 25 June, www.independent.co.uk/news/uk/politics/brexit-latest-news-updates-remain-twitter-muslim-racist-abuse-a7101491.html [last accessed 25 June 2016].

Suchman, L. (2012) 'Configuration', in C. Lury and N. Wakeford (eds), *Inventive Methods: The Happening of the Social*, London and New York: Routledge, pp. 49–60.

Syal, R. (2013) 'Anger at "go home" message to illegal migrants', *The Guardian*, 25 July, www.theguardian.com/uk-news/2013/jul/25/coalition-row-adverts-illegal-immigrants [last accessed 26 June 2016].

Toscano, A. (2012) 'Seeing it whole: staging totality in social theory and art', *The Sociological Review*, 60 (S1): 164–83.

Tyler, I. (2013) *Revolting Subjects: Social Abjection and Resistance in Neoliberal Britain*, London: Zed Books.

UNHCR (2016a) *Weekly Report – Europe's Refugee Emergency, 22 June 2016*, http://data.unhcr.org/mediterranean/download.php?id=1578 [last accessed 26 June 2016].

UNHCR (2016b) *Syria International Refugee Response, Inter-Agency Information Sharing Portal*, http://data.unhcr.org/syrianrefugees/regional.php [last accessed 30 April 2016].

UNPF (2016) *Migration* www.unfpa.org/migration# [last accessed 27 April 2016].

Vaughan-Williams, N. (2010) 'The UK border security continuum: Virtual biopolitics and the simulation of the sovereign ban', *Environment and Planning D: Society and Space*, 28 (6): 1071–83.

Walia, H. (2013) *Undoing Border Imperialism*, Edinburgh: AKPress/Institute for Anarchist Studies.

Walters, W. (2006) 'Border/Control', *European Journal of Social Theory*, 9 (2): 187–204.

Wetherell, M. (2012) *Affect and Emotion*, London: Sage Publications.

Wolff, S. (2008) 'Border management in the Mediterranean: Internal, external and ethical challenges', *Cambridge Review of International Affairs*, 21 (2): 253–71.

York, C. (2016) 'Post EU referendum racism documented online and it's really scary', *Huffington Post*, 26 June, www.huffingtonpost.co.uk/entry/eu-referendum-racism_uk_576fe161e4b08d2c56396075 [last accessed 26 June 2016].

Living Research One: Why are we doing this? Public sociology and public life

This short section is a conversation between an activist involved in the project[1] and a member of the research team. Each reflects candidly on the value of the MIC project to civil society and on social research (and socially engaged research) in general as a 'public good'.

Sukhwant: Personally, I was motivated to get involved in the Mapping Immigration Controversy project because of a sense of frustration with the way that immigration was being discussed by politicians and the media. There seemed to be a cross-party consensus on the need to restrict immigration. There was almost no public or media attention to the specific experiences of people subject to immigration controls. My personal engagement also carried an investment and commitment to anti-racism, a belief that as academics we have a role in highlighting discriminatory and dehumanising practices and policies and in challenging these. And conducting the AARX[2] surveys was a way to collate information about the experiences of local people and to engage them in a conversation about their views, which aren't always obvious – as we discovered at the last general

---

[1] Southall Black Sisters (SBS) is a not-for-profit organisation, established in 1979 to meet the needs of Black (Asian and African-Caribbean) women. It aims to highlight and challenge all forms of gender-related violence against women; and to empower women to gain more control over their lives, live without fear of violence and assert their human rights to justice, equality and freedom. SBS were our research partners, helping us with the fieldwork in Ealing and Hounslow.
[2] Action Against Racism and Xenophobia is a group of academics and activists who came together to conduct 'flash research' into the impacts of the Go Home vans, as a precursor to the Mapping Immigration Controversy research project.

election [2015], we tend to surround ourselves with others that hold similar views. What prompted Southall Black Sisters to want to participate in the AARX survey and then to become one of the community partners in the Mapping Immigration Controversy bid? And why did you think it would be valuable to involve the SBS support group in the focus group sessions?

Southall Black Sisters: The research was timely. For us, it was part of a process that had already started at SBS. The London borough of Ealing was one of the areas where the Go Home vans were piloted. Alongside that, women using the [Southall Black Sisters] centre were telling us about the stops and checks taking place at the local train station. We were hearing from them that there had been an increase in the number of immigration raids within the local area. So we were already discussing this with users of the centre. The research enabled the women to see their own experiences as connected to others around the country. Also, we saw our involvement in the research as part of our wider community work; it became a particularly good example of this. Immigration is a toxic issue and we know from the two public meetings that we then organised jointly with you and the MIC team that the local community is divided on this issue. After all, this is a deprived area and it is easy for people to blame each other. The research was one way of doing sustained community work, of flagging those divisions and challenging them. In a sense it was a form of community cohesion work[3] – whatever we might think of the government's cohesion agenda, when we are questioning and challenging divisions within local communities we are doing cohesion work. These events had a unifying effect, they enabled the coming together of people within local areas.

Sukhwant: You referred there to the users of your centre, can we talk a bit about their engagement with the fieldwork? I found it really enlightening, right through from the surveys to the focus groups to the public meetings. People had so much to say on this issue. And they supplied valuable insights into the incidence of immigration raids and stops and checks, including new information about people being stopped at particular bus stops and outside usual office hours, the sorts of times where ethnic minorities will be working the early morning, late evening or night shifts. Things we may have suspected but didn't know were happening. And I felt the data collated here

---

[3] 'Community cohesion' became important in UK local and national government from 2001, as an attempt to redefine 'multiculturalism' (see Jones, 2013).

[at the SBS centre], through the focus groups, gave rise to some of the key themes within the MIC findings, especially the point that the Home Office and media campaigns were exacerbating divisions within local communities and local people are distinguishing between immigrants that they consider to be deserving and undeserving of support.

Southall Black Sisters: Yes! If you remember, one of the focus group sessions was fairly coherent and women had the opportunity to share their personal experiences, fears and concerns and to support each other. And the focus group session gave them a voice, it allowed them to say for themselves the massive impact immigration rules were having on their daily lives. Up until then, there had not been many spaces to highlight these impacts or to record their daily lived experiences. But the second focus group session reflected local tensions and hostilities – there were lots of references to 'us' and 'them', points about the worthiness of some immigrants and not others. That second session took place in the context of heightened UKIP mobilisation against Eastern Europeans and some of that anti-Eastern European sentiment was expressed by participants in that session. For us, getting involved in the MIC research was part of a process, a continuation of work we were already doing with service users. And after the focus group sessions we continued some of those debates – as a follow-up to the points made at the second focus group, we organised a debate on the elections and political parties and we did a lot of work on building understanding and empathy towards all migrants, to encourage users of the centre to understand that anti-immigrant sentiment is not just impacting on them but on other communities as well.

Sukhwant: I do have a question in my mind though; even I as a researcher wonder how much impact we have actually had, beyond awareness raising and discussion among the research participants. The European elections [2014] and the subsequent national election results [2015] seem to have wholeheartedly supported the anti-immigrant hostility of that period. And here in the UK, the government did bring in the Immigration Act 2014, irrespective of opposition and projects like ours giving voice to their divisive and undemocratic nature. And, although the two public meetings in Southall were really well attended and we had an excellent discussion, I had the sense that we were talking to the 'already converted'. There were just two voices that contrasted with what speakers on the panel were saying – the man at the first meeting that wanted to make a strong distinction between recent migrants allegedly claiming welfare benefits and the work ethic of his parents' generation. Then there was the man at the second meeting, where we discussed the MIC project findings, who said he could not understand why a focus on 'illegal' immigrants would impact on established ethnic minority communities. But these were minority views at the public meetings. Did you see any value in these events and what is your sense of the impact that we had?

Southall Black Sisters: But it gave us space to make the connections. For example, to hear from the JCWI [Joint Council for the Welfare of Immigrants] speaker about the work going on in Birmingham around landlord checks. We heard about the rise and fight across the country as well as the compliance. You make connections and build support, solidarity among dissenting voices. We heard about the disparate ways that people are protesting. In fact our contact with Rita Chadha[4] came through all this. None of us were aware of Rita's fantastic work and she is such an important voice. Also, we can't look at 'impact' as something that will completely overhaul all these things. The anti-immigrant push is like a juggernaut! It has been layer upon layer of anti-immigration measures. Some of the measures in the current Crime Bill are like the pass laws of apartheid South Africa – if this goes through, it will allow the police to stop people not just on suspicion that you might not legally be in this country but to ask for your documents and if you can't produce them within the stipulated time then be able to arrest you. They don't even have to have reasonable suspicion, just suspicion.

Sukhwant: So even more likely to involve racial profiling.

Southall Black Sisters: Yes. And you don't even have to give a good reason. The combination of this and the new measures under the Immigration Act have created levels of fear among people because landlords etc. are being encouraged to report people. So in that climate, where minorities are treading on eggshells, all of this work is so, so important because it's about trying to create alternative networks. The anti-immigrant push is a tidal wave, it's a juggernaut!

---

[4] Throughout the MIC research project Rita Chadha was Chief Executive of RAMFEL (Refugee And Migrant Forum of Essex and London). RAMFEL was a community partner for the research in Barking and Dagenham. Prior to the research project, Rita was a prominent voice opposing the Go Home van in local and national media and active in the AARX survey (see note [2]), and RAMFEL supported one of their clients to make a successful legal challenge to the Go Home van initiative (see Taylor, Gidda and Syal, 2013).

And all we can do is create spaces for discussion and networks that challenge those views. One other very real impact is that the next time when one of the women in the focus group sees an Eastern European she won't be so hardened in her views.

Sukhwant: Did it do that? Did it change the views of the women within the groups?

Southall Black Sisters: Yes, yes. We were doing the Everyday Borders project[5] at the same time and that helped as well. That period, the series of discussions, was a good opening for us to discuss what all of us, local people can do. And it was important for creating alternative networks of support. Networks are vital, not only for individual women to overcome some of their fears and sense of isolation, but also for us as an organisation to link with other groups working around the country.

Sukhwant: Is that why SBS are involved in a number of social research projects?

Southall Black Sisters: Yes but there is a reason that this particular project has been unique – we are not encouraging, carte blanche, all academics to come and knock on our door [laughs]. This project was unique because women had already had a spontaneous protest outside the Himalaya Palace and then organised a demonstration outside the reception centre in Hounslow. These actions helped to galvanise individual feelings into a collective sentiment. It focused attention on a pressing issue. It generated a public debate. And that is the context in which the research comes along. It's not like the research has manufactured something. It's not like the research, or SBS workers for that matter, are manufacturing it. We were all supporting women that wanted to do something about it. And the research offered to map what was happening around the country. And it also gave us spaces for self-reflection. Activism teaches research what the issues are but academics may help us understand the processes and to develop our analysis of all this. That self-reflection is always a necessary part of activism. Research gives you a chance to step back and think about what has gone on, to connect your input with what other people are doing around the country. But it doesn't work when researchers just swan in, in an instrumental way. We have

---

[5] Research conducted at the University of East London between 2013 and 2016 as part of the EU Borderscapes project; see Yuval-Davis, Wemyss and Cassidy, 2016.

that experience all the time, where academics just want us to organise the focus groups and ask the women to discuss a particular issue, without context or process, then it becomes manufactured. And there is also the question of payment.

Sukhwant: You've raised two issues there. So the research needs to be part of a process. And two, the financial aspects – are you saying that payment is an important part of this discussion?

Southall Black Sisters: One, staff time and staff resources that are taken up when we engage with research and that needs to be recognised. Secondly, it's the women's time and researchers need to recognise that they don't have any money, especially those subject to immigration controls. Researchers tend to think they can just come along and do this session and take the data and go away and write up. But the women need to be reimbursed, as they were on this project. The fact that they are giving up their time and they are travelling in especially, all this needs to be taken into account. But the other thing that happened, and this is an important offshoot that has made this research project unique, is that the same women then decided to get involved in UEL [University of East London]'s Everyday Borders project and that process that they started on the MIC project continued. That was really empowering, it helped their confidence and a couple eventually went on to speak at public events about their experiences.

Sukhwant: That is great to hear! The focus groups were so powerful, really comprehensive discussions. I can see how your activism and the data have contributed to the project but have you learned or gained anything from us?

Southall Black Sisters: We can say for sure that being part of this helped us to reflect on what was happening. We spoke at a couple of the events and two of us also co-authored the *New Left Project* blogs with you and Yasmin.[6] And we valued the joint production of these intellectual outputs – that is real partnership, not parachuting in collating data and exiting again. And I'll tell you what that helped us to do, it helped us to develop our own thinking – key points that we aired for the first time at the Westminster Breakfast Briefing.[7] It

---

[6] Dhaliwal and Patel, 2015; Gunaratnam and Patel, 2015.
[7] An event held by the MIC project to share our interim research findings with policy-makers and activists in March 2015, at which Pragna Pratel from SBS gave a response to the findings and the ongoing research.

helped us articulate the view that this drive on immigration, this 'hostile environment' (and all the duties being foisted on statutory agencies and local people), this drive contradicts the protection principle and public policy/practice guidelines that remind public sector workers that they have a duty to protect women and children from violence and abuse. We had been thinking and discussing these points but the spaces around the project helped us to consolidate some of that thinking. And in fact the research project bolstered the position of SBS as well. Campaigning on immigration, in Southall particularly, has historically been led by BME [Black and Minority Ethnic] men while there have been few voices from the women's voluntary sector questioning and challenging immigration rules. For us, getting involved in that space was important and the research project gave us legitimacy in this respect – we were involved in the work, so no one could say 'well who are you, how do you know what is going on?' And the events embedded our group in community structures and processes. And it's really important that people can see a women's group playing a part in the networks and spaces that have arisen as a consequence of the range of activities that are challenging the intensification of anti-immigrant policies and views. This is as important for migrant rights networks to see this as it is for other women's groups to see. And for each section to connect the issues across race and gender and class. Women's groups like Sandhya's group – Sisters 4 Safety – in Manchester have felt isolated and academia can play a role in countering that isolation by linking them into what else is happening around the country.

Has reading this conversation made you think any differently about how academic researchers might work with community and activist groups? If so, in what ways?

When planning a research collaboration between academic researchers and community or activist groups, what issues might you consider with regard to:

1 Benefits of the relationship (to the community or activist group, to the participants, to the researcher)
2 Costs of the relationship (to the community or activist group, to the participants, to the researcher)
3 Ethics
4 Relationships
5 Clarity of roles
6 What happens after the fieldwork finishes?

References

Dhaliwal, S. and Patel, M. (2015) 'Hostility and dissent: Experiencing anti-immigrant messaging', *New Left Project*, 13 July, www.newleftproject.org/index.php/site/article_comments/hostility_and_dissent_experiencing_anti_immigrant_messaging [last accessed 20 May 2016].

Gunaratnam, Y. and Patel, P. (2015) 'The hypocrisy of immigration politics: Compassion at a distance', *New Left Project*, 20 April, www.newleftproject.org/index.php/site/article_comments/the_hypocrisy_of_immigration_politics_compassion_at_a_distance [last accessed 20 May 2016].

Jones, H. (2013) *Negotiating Cohesion, Inequality and Change: Uncomfortable Positions in Local Government*, Bristol: Policy Press.

Taylor, M., Gidda, M. and Syal, R. (2013) ' "Go home" ad campaign targeting illegal immigrants faces court challenge', *The Guardian*, 26 July, www.theguardian.com/uk-news/2013/jul/26/go-home-ad-campaign-court-challenge [last accessed 20 May 2016].

Yuval-Davis, N., Wemyss, G. and Cassidy, K. (2016) 'Changing the racialized "common sense" of everyday bordering', *Open Democracy*, 17 February, www.opendemocracy.net/uk/nira-yuval-davis-georgie-wemyss-kathryn-cassidy/changing-racialized-common-sense-of-everyday-bord [last accessed 20 May 2016].

2

Permeable borders, performative politics and public mistrust

Rita: I was just taking the train from Victoria to Clapham Junction. And Clapham Junction when I get off from the train, I saw so many UKBA [UK Border Agency] people they were there, I saw them with large dogs, blocking the entire area. I had a visa and have it now also. But I got really scared because I could see the place blocked. I cannot describe how terrified I was, wondering why there is a man there with dogs and searching, what are they searching, was it drugs, or what? I got so panicked and scared that I went and sat in the wrong train ... When I got on the train I started crying. I was thinking how long will I live with this fear? I'm not allowed to work ... I started to think to myself, if I can't move around at all, that people are blocking the way like this, and I'm so scared then perhaps suicide is better.

(Ealing and Hounslow Focus Group,
conducted by Sukhwant)

Our [Go Home poster] campaign targets illegal immigrants without any discrimination at all between them. By no stretch of the rational imagination can it be described as 'racist'. Furthermore, the campaign is not meant to, and does not, discourage legal immigrants who have earned the right to live or settle in Britain. To claim that the poster campaign is unfair to legal migrants is silly.

(Mark Harper, Immigration Minister,
writing in the *Daily Mail*, 2013)

Alan: Yes, they're trying to give the impression that they're doing something about it ... 'We are doing our job, we are catching these illegals, we are putting them in the van and we're taking them to the jail' and half an hour later they're going to let them go again, they're not saying that bit, are they?

(Dagenham Focus Group, conducted by Yasmin)

The three statements above provide very different perspectives on the performative politics of immigration control, demonstrating some of the contradictory reactions to the increasing visibility of the 'toughness' of UK immigration enforcement. In the first narrative, a woman describes the visceral fear that gripped her on seeing a large, public show of force by border officials at a domestic railway station in South London. Rita had a valid visa and therefore in theory had no reason to fear being stopped. But she was 'terrified', 'panicked', 'scared' and 'nervous', to the extent that she got on the wrong train, and began to think that death might be better than such constant fear when simply trying to move around the city. She saw her way, and perhaps her life, as 'blocked', almost impossible.

This account is in contrast to the second extract, in which the then Minister for Immigration, Mark Harper MP, makes a defence of the Go Home vans in a column in the *Daily Mail* newspaper (see also Introduction). He argues that it is not 'rational' to view the poster as threatening to anyone other than people who are in contravention of immigration law. By extension it seems that Harper would class the experience of terror described by Rita as 'silly' too. Why should Rita feel 'blocked' if she is carrying a valid visa and being 'rational'?

In the final extract, the speaker identified himself in our focus group as supporting the far-right British National Party (BNP), a party which has long supported 'voluntary resettlement' for (legal) 'immigrants *and their descendants*' (BNP, 2010; our emphasis). Much journalistic commentary and analysis of the Go Home vans suggested that their purpose was to appeal as much to this audience – the voter sceptical about immigration and turning to far-right parties – as to those 'in the UK illegally' (see BBC, 2013; Merrick, 2013; Wigmore, 2013). This was a view supported by some of our interviews with policy insiders about the reasons for the rise in demonstrations of toughness in government communications about immigration (see Chapter 3). Talking not just about the Go Home vans but also about the images of arrests by immigration enforcement officers circulated by the Home Office on Twitter and elsewhere, Alan both supports the idea that such performances reach out to these audiences, and questions their efficacy in doing so. The message is at once recognised and dismissed as insufficient and as a public relations game. It seems, indeed, that by following the logic circulating in Westminster, whereby government has given up on trying to discuss the facts of immigration in favour of emotional appeals to reassurance and fear (see Chapter 3), the Home Office has met with further scepticism.

In what follows, we explore these different experiences and viewpoints, focusing on the ways in which the theatricalised performances of the state emerged in the particular moment of border control materialised by Operation Vaken. Through our research we have been able to delve into the effects of the state performance and mobilisation of the border through the accounts of both those who have suffered the most coercive aspects of bordering and those who are most vocal in their distrust of political elites. In both groups, the performative aspect of Home Office immigration campaigns is identified as a moment of crisis and crumbling credibility. What should be constitutive becomes indicative of an underlying lack; and for both of these audiences this serves to confirm the vulnerability and contradictions of government activity in this area. In our discussion of these complicated dynamics, we will consider the responses of different audiences to highly staged instances of Home Office performance, suggesting that, in the process, what is revealed is the scepticism of these varied audiences towards the performativity of immigration enforcement and its politics.

In making sense of these different entanglements in the performance of immigration enforcement, in this chapter we:

1   engage with debates about performative politics to consider the apparently contradictory performances mounted in the name of border control
2   discuss the deployment of theatricalised violence by the state
3   argue that performances of state power should be understood as directed at several audiences and also as techniques that segment the population
4   consider how some attempts to address a diversity of audiences can be met with scepticism, anxiety or indifference
5   note how, despite amplified expressions of anti-migrant sentiment across public life, the anti-migrant performances of government are viewed with suspicion and re-interpreted through a popular scepticism influenced by a broader culture of 'anti-politics'.[1]

Performing coercion

The key question that concerned us during Operation Vaken was a deceptively simple one: how do governments seek to demonstrate that

---

[1] By 'anti-politics' we are referring to both feelings of disaffection and disillusionment and to the movement of political activities and interventions outside of established political institutions and spaces.

they are controlling immigration? Importantly, although the Go Home vans might be regarded as the most crass and obvious form of political performance, throughout the course of the project we came to understand the many other and varied forms political performance can take. For example, while we were doing our research the Home Office initiated a series of interventions, all designed to confirm the government's commitment to tough border controls. The majority of these constituted what we might understand as speech acts.[2] These were public proclamations of intent. At the same time, there was a period during the project when the more overt coercion of immigration raids and people being 'lifted' in public places seemed to escalate. In trying to better understand the impact of the varied initiatives undertaken to create a 'hostile environment', we sought out responses to this range of quite different actions. We have now come to understand both the communication campaigns and the physical assertion of the border through checks, raids, detentions and deportations as modes of state performance.

Central to our interests has been the manner in which popular understandings of sovereignty place the issue of the border as a central test and marker of sovereign power. Nicholas Vaughan-Williams, a scholar in politics and international relations, explains the centrality of border marking to theoretical accounts of the exercise of state sovereignty:

> the concept of the border of the state can be said to frame the limits of sovereign power as something supposedly contained within fixed territorially demarcated parameters.
>
> (Vaughan-Williams, 2009: 730)

Alongside these assumptions about the role of the border in demonstrating sovereign power and for complex reasons that may be particular to the UK, the question of immigration control has become

---

[2] The philosopher J.L. Austin (1975/1962), known for his pioneering work on 'Speech Act Theory', makes a distinction between the 'illocutionary' speech act that does what it sets out to do in the moment and the 'perlocutionary' component of 'utterances' that has impacts beyond the moment of interaction. However, as the feminist philosopher Judith Butler (1997) has pointed out, in reality this distinction is hard to maintain. Whatever the intention, any speech act might spin out to become perlocutionary. What is said may come to circulate more widely and in a longer timeframe, and in this process, other responses and interpretations can proliferate.

one of the central talismanic markers of the alleged failure of main-stream politics. In the moment of increasingly vocalised anti-politics in the UK, the issue of immigration has taken on a symbolic status that goes far beyond the detail of any policy intervention or outcome. While we will go on to reveal the extent to which 'the UK' is a diverse space in relation to the reception of government-led immigration campaigns (see Chapter 4), the presentation of the issue of immigration in mainstream political and media discourse erases many of these differences. For the most part then, immigration is presented as: a test of sovereignty and/or as evidence that sovereignty has been eroded; an example of the diverging interests of a (possibly metropolitan)[3] political class and the rest of the population; an indication of the overall loss of control of central government; a demonstration of the questionable use of data in official pronouncements. The chapters in this volume will go on to reflect on the repercussions of these varying views among different audiences, including the manner in which such discourses position different actors as inside or outside political space.

In relation to the exclusions that arise from border marking, Vaughan-Williams has revisited the philosophy of Giorgio Agamben (1998, 1999, 2005) to think again about the spaces of indistinction and what Agamben calls the 'banned' person. In doing this, Vaughan-Williams reopens debates about the location and character of sovereign power and, importantly for our interests here, the ambiguous and ambivalent inclusion extended to those who are disallowed by the exercise of power. As we will go on to explain, these discussions of the banned and disallowed person have been important in helping us to acknowledge and interpret the unexpected and contradictory impacts of immigration enforcement campaigns for the (more usually) ignored subject of border enforcement (namely irregular migrants, refugees and asylum seekers).

Our aim then is to offer a critical reading of the performance of recent border enforcement campaigns in order to understand the impact of such campaigns on political spaces and popular understandings of the business of government. To do this, we will link our analysis of state campaigns to a larger debate about the conduct of political life and suggest that the assertion of power may not always

---

[3] The term 'metropolitan elite' has been used by the media and politicians across the political spectrum not only to denote the class privilege of liberal Londoners but also as a way of suggesting that the views of this elite group are out of touch with the feelings and experiences of 'ordinary people' (see Chapter 6).

play out in linear or predictable ways among the wider population. In particular, we have been alert to the debates about anti-politics or postpolitics (see Burnham, 2002; Hay, 2007; Schedler, 1997) signifying a disaffection, negativity or a disengagement from political institutions and processes, such as elections (see Saunders, 2014). Yet these ideas have been rarely linked to discussions of immigration and state immigration campaigns.

Our exploration of state performances in the name of immigration control found that the fear of popular scepticism both informed government tactics and circulated in the reception of the various campaign initiatives. This constant whisper of scepticism in the face of all and any government initiatives relating to immigration control brings up questions of political performance and the impact of such performances.

What do we mean by political performance?

Shirin Rai offers a useful framework through which to analyse political performances and the ways in which they are received and interpreted by different audiences. For Rai, political performances are:

> those performances that seek to communicate to an audience meaning-making related to state institutions, policies and discourses. This meaning-making is read in very specific socio-political contexts; it can be either consolidative or challenging of the dominant narratives of politics.
>
> (Rai, 2015: 1179–80)

Rai's interest is in the active and planned business of political life. Her own work has examined parliamentary ritual and how this positions women. When she writes of political performance, it is with a focus on statecraft and the actions of political representatives. It is a conception that places most of us as audience, not actor, but in a manner that gives due weight to the interpretative power of audiences:

> Its legitimacy rests on a convincing performance; it has to be representative of a particular political stand; it must engage the audience that is its particular target; it should satisfy the formal rules, rituals and conventions of the institutions through which the meaning is being projected; and be received as logical and coherent. Because much of this performance can be challenged by disruption of the performance itself through counter-performance, mis-recognition

or mis-reading of and by the audience, political performance is inherently unstable and vulnerable to being seen as illegitimate.

(Rai, 2015: 1180)

The central realisation here is the inherent instability of political performance. Much of what we found suggested that various audiences viewed government performances as weak or misplaced and, as a result of this reading, were confirmed in their view of the incompetence or irrelevance of government more generally. The inherent instability of political performance is of key importance when considering recent immigration campaigns because this reminds us that what the powerful say and do may not determine how all actors understand what is happening in public space. With this in mind, we have used Rai's work to inform our readings of this set of state performances. Rai suggests a framework for understanding the production of political performances by identifying two axes of activity:

On one axis we can map the markers of representation: the body, the space/place, words/script/speech and performative labour. Together, these four markers encapsulate political performance. On the second axis we can map the effects of performance: authenticity, mode of representation, liminality and resistance (of and to) political representation.

(Rai, 2015: 1181)

Applying this schema to Home Office immigration campaigns in the period of our project has allowed us to pull out the aspects of these campaigns that typify these particular strands of performance. Therefore, we might consider that bodies are adapted, rebranded or contained through the varied activities of updating uniforms and instituting immigration raids (see also Bunyan, 1985: 295). The performance of immigration control utilises space and place both by reiterating the border at the border and through new signage in public locations such as hospital waiting rooms (see Figure 2). Equally the circulation of immigration enforcement teams, branded vans and public raids all extend the space of political performance to the street and this also is a tactical remaking of political space (Yuval-Davis, Wemyss and Cassidy, 2016). As we have already identified, much of the campaigning activity under scrutiny consists of speech acts, including tweets, slogans and branding. As these performances are not tied to any particular representative, the performative labour can be harder to identify. However, the positioning of journalists as an

Figure 2: Signs in NHS on limited rights to healthcare for some migrants

internal audience to the most coercive elements of border control through invitations to witness its performance, along with the overall effort of communication and will to embody authority, all point to the locations of performative labour in these endeavours. We have understood the campaigns that we analysed as representing this range of tactical performances.

Alongside focus groups, interviews and observations in our own six research locations, to help us understand how the wider population reacted to these campaigns, we commissioned a survey from Ipsos MORI on attitudes to Home Office immigration campaigns (see the Appendix for more details). The opening section of the survey mapped public awareness of a number of overlapping initiatives, chosen to represent the focus on *communicating* the active pursuit of immigration control. The survey asked people whether they were aware of the following:

1   advertising vans around London in 2013 stating 'In the UK illegally? GO HOME OR FACE ARREST'
2   tweets from the Home Office showing images of people being detained by immigration officers and the hashtag #immigrationoffender
3   journalists accompanying immigration officers on raids of wedding ceremonies, homes or workplaces
4   signs in NHS premises stating 'NHS hospital treatment is not free for everyone' [see Figure 2]
5   UK Border branded signs about immigration regulations at passport control areas introduced in 2006
6   uniforms for passport control officers introduced in 2006/7
7   Immigration Enforcement branded vans on UK streets
8   other communications (please specify)
9   none of these
10 don't know.

We wanted to map the extent of public knowledge of the Home Office campaigns and also to get a sense of how it felt to be positioned as an audience to these campaigns. In effect, we conducted a very basic form of audience research and, in so doing, we sought to shift the discussion away from attitudes to a thing called 'immigration', and towards an assessment of how government campaigns about immigration made sense or incited sensation for different audiences. Table 1 summarises some key outcomes of the survey we commissioned from Ipsos MORI.

After the heightened publicity accompanying the Go Home vans, it is perhaps surprising that such small proportions of the sample were aware of the Vaken initiatives. The media coverage of the Go Home vans was intensive for a short period of time, yet by the time of our survey more than a year later only a little more than a quarter (26 per cent) of those surveyed recalled this campaign. Other initiatives also had little impact on popular recall; only new signage at passport control elicited a higher level of recognition (31 per cent). In relation to the introduction of vans (either the ad-van or those used by enforcement officers), tweets or accompanying journalists, those who said that they were aware of various initiatives were almost as likely – or more likely – to be concerned about the impact of unnecessary suspicion as they were to be reassured by evidence of government action. The areas where a significantly greater proportion expressed a sense

Table 1: Awareness and responses to Home Office communication campaigns on immigration (%) (see Appendix for sample and methodological details)

Home office activity	Proportion aware of this activity	Of those who are aware, those who feel 'reassured that the government is taking action against irregular/illegal immigration'	Of those who are aware, those who feel 'concerned that some people are being treated with unnecessary suspicion in everyday situations'
Advertising vans around London in 2013 stating 'In the UK illegally? Go Home or Face Arrest'	26 (n=603)	28	34
Tweets from the Home Office showing images of people being detained by immigration officers and the hashtag #immigrationoffender	6 (n=145)	20	33
Journalists accompanying immigration officers on raids of wedding ceremonies, homes or workplaces	13 (n=317)	31	26
Signs in NHS premises stating 'NHS hospital treatment is not free for everyone'	20 (n=474)	41	19
UK Border branded signs about immigration regulations at passport control areas introduced in 2006	31 (n=715)	41	18
Uniforms for passport control officers introduced in 2006/2007	23 (n=522)	41	13
Immigration Enforcement branded vans on UK streets	18 (n=426)	31	28

of reassurance – NHS signs, border signs and uniforms for border staff – relate more concretely to the marking of a static border albeit extended into the space of healthcare. As Rai (2015) has indicated, the sense of space and place significantly shapes the possibilities and impact of political performance. In our case, the spaces in which the 'performance' is enacted appears to shape the extent to which the general audience considers it legitimate.

The Ipsos MORI survey also gave respondents opportunities to provide textual, qualitative responses in addition to the multiple-choice questions. Although this option was taken only by a minority of those familiar with the government campaigns, the responses show the uncertain impact of the performance (see Table 2). In order to summarise this range of material, we have organised comments in relation to each campaign strand under the headings of:

- considered ineffective
- opposition/disgust
- agreement with approach
- stupid or equivalent
- a failed or misplaced performance
- other responses.

Table 2: 'Other' written responses to the question 'Which, if any, of the following best reflects how you feel about this communication/action?' (responses are verbatim as typed by survey respondents)

Advertising vans around London in 2013 stating 'In the UK illegally? Go Home or Face Arrest'	
Considered ineffective	'i feel strongly that the previous labour govt + coalition have performed badly in controlling immigration'
	'government doing nothing'
	'i think the vans are a waste of money on a personal note. we need to curb immigration to uk & i now vote for UKIP as a protest vote'
	'The Home Office are not doing enough to combat immigration ie funding reduced to tackle this major issue'
	'they have to control immigration so i am for the work of officers but against the vans as they create problems for us british citizens with our neighbours'
	'the vans are a waste of public money'
	'CANNOT SEE VANS BEING THE ANSWER.'

Opposition/disgust	'A worrying shift to the right wing in this country' 'Disgusted by it' I think it's horribly racist.' 'Angry' '1930's Berlin?' 'Absolutely fucking outraged that public funds were spent on such a crass and insensitive waste of effort' 'Intimidating!' 'i think the vans initiative in london is appalling'
Agreement with approach	'the illegals are here on false pretences & should be deported immediately.' 'where there is a strong suspicion'
Stupid or equivalent	'Ridiculus' 'ed embarrass' 'It was stupid'
A failed or misplaced performance	'counter productive' 'bad publicity!' 'inappropriate action'
Other responses	'ON TV' 'i am fully aware of the immigration problem'

Tweets from the Home Office showing images of people being detained by immigration officers and the hashtag #immigrationoffender

Considered ineffective	*NONE*
Opposition/disgust	'disgusted'
Agreement with approach	'fine'
Stupid or equivalent	*NONE*
A failed or misplaced performance	*NONE*
Other responses	*NONE*

Signs in NHS premises stating 'NHS hospital treatment is not free for everyone'

Considered ineffective	'they need to act more not just put up signs'
Opposition/disgust	'Disgusted' 'should not be there' 'legal immagrints should get free nhs'
Agreement with approach	'foreigners abusing our nhs' 'Fine'

Stupid or equivalent	NONE
A failed or misplaced performance	'its not necessarily immigration.its not being legal or illegal.'
Other responses	'only concerned about postcadev treatment'

UK Border branded signs about immigration regulations at passport control areas introduced in 2006

Considered ineffective	'not enough is being done' 'should be stricter' 'I feel thst these signs would make little difference - I doubt anybody intending to enter the country illegally is going to be discouraged by signs.' 'theres not enough resources'
Opposition/disgust	NONE
Agreement with approach	'Fine' 'concerned some may be treated with uneccesary suspicion as well as too many immigrants entering.'
Stupid or equivalent	NONE
A failed or misplaced performance	NONE
Other responses	NONE

Journalists accompanying immigration officers on raids of wedding ceremonies, homes or workplaces

Considered ineffective	'Steps taken not enough'
Opposition/disgust	'Outraged' 'Disgusted'
Agreement with approach	'Fine with it' 'too much immigration'
Stupid or equivalent	NONE
A failed or misplaced performance	'dont feel the need for it to be publisised' 'it is an inappropiate way of carrying out government bussiness'
Other responses	'Null'

Uniforms for passport control officers introduced in 2006/7

Considered ineffective	'theres not enough resources'
Opposition/disgust	NONE

Agreement with approach	'Fine' 'it makes the process formal and tidy.nothing to do with illegal immigrants.it makes them look professional.its same in other countries.'
Stupid or equivalent	NONE
A failed or misplaced performance	'thought they were badly fitting - not good impression'
Other responses	'More widespread than PEOPLE realise'

Immigration Enforcement branded vans on UK streets

Considered ineffective	'government is not taking enough action' 'money would be better spent tracking down illegals' 'dont feel gov't is taking enough action' 'waste of money' 'it creates the wrong impression of the weakness of the immigration service'
Opposition/disgust	'xenophobic, alarmist,unprofessional, unethical.' 'feel digraceful' 'Disgusted' 'they are a disgrce' 'UNFAIR/ILLEGAL' 'CONCERNED ABOUT THEM FUELLING RACISM' 'FEEL SAD ABOUT THE SITUATION SURROUNDING ILLEGAL IMMIGRATES' 'Offensive' 'Racist'
Agreement with approach	'like it' 'If it's done in a good way then that's a good thing'
Stupid or equivalent	'it's a joke'
A failed or misplaced performance	'govt are doing their best' 'badly phrased' 'legal immigrants may be victimised'
Other responses	'bigger problem than government thinks'

The question of the effects of the performance of immigration enforcement has been central for us. From the very beginnings of the project we have tried both to describe the particularity of these interventions at a time of heightened politicisation of immigration control and to register and trace the impact of such actions on migrants and on others. In the process, our analyses have revealed the extent to which campaign messages circulate differently according to audience and location. With this in mind, the questions that are raised by Rai in relation to the effects of performance should be regarded as varying across audiences. The second axis that Rai identifies consists of:

- Authenticity – Is this for real? Vocal scepticism reveals distrust of performance and effectivity of state actions overall (e.g. 'Absolutely fucking outraged that public funds were spent on such a crass and insensitive waste of effort').
- Mode of representation – for vans, this mode has been regarded as improper and/or ineffective. For signage, there seems to be a greater acceptance of both script and place (e.g. 'they need to act more not just put up signs').
- Liminality – possibility of rupture, here arising from dangerous admission that performance is required (e.g. 'it creates the wrong impression of the weakness of the immigration service').
- Resistance of/to political representation – including humour, ridicule, outright disbelief (e.g. 'it's a joke').

All four of these aspects of reception were mentioned in the sceptical readings of state campaigns in our survey. In particular scepticism was sometimes expressed as ridicule and the performances were also taken as a reminder that authority is uncertain and sometimes ineffective (see also Living Research Five). Taken together the two axes allow us to consider political performance both as a set of performative *techniques* and as a set of *responses* or audiences.

It is important to remember that the immigration campaigns that we studied did not inhabit the usual spaces of political life and did not constitute the ritualistic performances of bodies such as those seen in Parliament. Instead, they were designed to enact and mark the border in everyday locations. At the same time, the very act of reasserting such sovereign authority also served to reveal the fragility and precariousness of state power. As Rai points out, political performances are always inherently unstable and open to alternative interpretations. The very act of seeking to make power visible can be regarded as a sign of weakness (because 'real power' has no need of such theatrical assertions) or as a demystification of the workings of power (revealing the secrets that create the illusion of authority).

Immigration campaigns that took place during our research were undertaken against a backdrop of public scepticism and the increasingly amplified view that government had no control over immigration. We learned from discussions with those tasked with the formation of policy and government campaigns that public opinion was considered to be beyond influence by any data that could be presented to demonstrate 'effective border control' (discussed further in Chapter 3). In this context, the performative assertions that the border is being guarded can be seen as an attempt to persuade the public that something is being done about immigration enforcement. The move to these particular modes of political performance is a response to the ineffectiveness of more usual practices of presenting evidence. Our task becomes, then, to understand the workings of government messages that are not presentations of evidence and to explore how such messages are received and interpreted by different audiences.

Popular scepticism

In our research, the most explicitly voiced scepticism came from those who identified themselves as wishing to see more and stronger controls on immigration. In Barking and Dagenham (a borough in the east of London), focus group discussion revolved around the negative impact of recent immigration in local neighbourhoods, yet these groups also expressed high levels of distrust in government initiatives to communicate actions taken as part of immigration control.

In Dagenham, one man revealed that he had stood for election as a BNP candidate – an action that had led to considerable public barracking. For this group, mainstream politics (national *and* local, as they were keen to point out) was out of touch with people like themselves and unable to address the issue of immigration in any meaningful way. In the context of these views, government communications on migration control, and the Go Home vans in particular, were interpreted as another distraction from the underlying impotence or indifference of government in relation to the issue of immigration control.

To understand the manner in which this form of scepticism is voiced, it is helpful to listen closely to the conversation. The first cause of scepticism arises from the purported audience for the 'Go Home' message. In assessing the impact, this group do not include themselves as part of the intended audience and point instead to the likely resistance from the implied audience.

> Yasmin: So with things like the van, what sort of impact do you think it actually has?
> Joe: None, because they don't take no notice anyway, they just wait until they get caught, you know that, don't you? What, you think

someone's going to hand theirself in, look, I'm a criminal, I just robbed a bank.

Carol: Not when it's paved with gold, no, they ain't going to hand themselves in.

(Dagenham Focus Group, conducted by Yasmin)

However, this unambiguous assertion of the ineffectiveness of the initiative contrasts with a point made earlier in the conversation. In an earlier remark, it had been suggested both that the offer made on the vans was welcome to those who wish to see fewer immigrants in Britain and that the offer of advice and support was magnanimous and should be regarded as such (echoed in the views of a policy-maker quoted in the next chapter).

Yasmin: So you're sort of saying different things. So on the one hand you're saying it's good because it's advising and on the other hand you're saying it's going to have no impact at all?

Joe: No, it's not going to have no impact, it's good for the people that live here.

Alan: Yeah.

Joe: It'll make them happy.

(Dagenham Focus Group, conducted by Yasmin)

These statements suggest that 'the people who live here' (i.e. non-migrants) will be made happy by the circulation of the vans and the publicity given to government immigration advice. Local residents become the intended audience and the performance takes on a different intention, to evoke the emotion of happiness. The feminist cultural theorist Sara Ahmed has outlined a way of understanding such shifting investments in 'happiness':

An attachment to happiness as a lost object involves not simply a form of mourning but also an anxiety that the wrong people can be happy, and even a desire for happiness to be returned to the right people.

(Ahmed, 2010: 13)

For a moment it seems that those in our focus group participate in these feelings of properly returned happiness, viewing the vans as a momentary confirmation that they have been listened to. Yet this lull passes quickly and the conversation moves back to the question of why the vans were withdrawn.

Alan: But the fact is, though, it made an impact, didn't it, because who said that it was racist, all the foreigners, all the foreigners revolted and said we're not having that.

Carol: Yeah, all the English said it's racist.

Alan: And that's the impact that it made, it brought the foreigners out to say we're not having that, that is racist against us and therefore the government went for them again and said you've got to take it off.

(Dagenham Focus Group, conducted by Yasmin)

In this final analysis of the vans, the idea that the intended audience is elsewhere returns. There is an obvious confusion about who initiated the campaign and who holds authority – 'the government … said you've got to take it off' as a result of supporting foreigners and the complaint of racism. There is also some variance between the two speakers – is it foreigners or the English who said it was racist? However, the overall sense of deflation is palpable. After the momentary happiness of being heard, the reminder that the impact has been to reaffirm the illegality of overt racism places this group outside the circuit of communication again.

The scepticism continued in the response to tweeted images of immigration raids. Here the same group explain why they place little trust in such images:

Joe: they've obviously raided somewhere and found a couple of illegals and they've taken them into custody, but what brings to mind again is what I said before, they won't keep them in custody, they'll give them bail to appear in court or to report to the police station every Tuesday or whatever and they won't be seen again.

(Dagenham Focus Group, conducted by Yasmin)

As discussed in the opening of the chapter, this process of Home Office reporting was considered disingenuous by this group. This was an issue that arose again later in the same discussion.

Alan: I've seen this on the television, on the police programmes where they've raided certain shops and things like that and they've arrested four or five and within a couple of days they've all been released to report back to the station, every week.

There was a strong sense in the group that the theatricality of such performances was designed to distract public attention from government weakness in the face of immigration.

Alan: They're trying to give the idea to the general public that they're doing something about it, but they're doing absolutely nothing.

Carol: Nothing, yeah.

Alan: Because they're going to release them people.

Joe: That van ain't big enough, though, is it?

> (Dagenham Focus Group, conducted by Yasmin)

Here the agreement within the group that such images are just for show reveals, paradoxically, that the government is not doing anything ('absolutely nothing'). The group agree that these campaigns are unconvincing to them, but that they may work for other, more trusting (gullible), audiences.

In Barking, discussion of the vans and tweets took a slightly different turn, returning to the question of what government hoped to achieve through such initiatives. The discussion opened with scepticism:

Annie: It's not going to work, because if you're illegal you're illegal and you're hiding, because you don't come out in society, you stay hidden, so yeah, it's true, it is true, but it's not going to work, I don't think. I don't object to the actual picture.

> (Barking Focus Group, conducted by Yasmin)

There is another circling around the question of the identity of the intended audience in this extract. Of note is how Annie clarifies that she is not offended ('I don't object'), so that she is not aligned with those complaining of racism. Instead, her concern is directed to the effectivity of this approach ('it's not going to work'). Annie assumes that she (and people like her) are not the primary intended audience; that role belongs to the 'illegal'. Yet the intended interlocutor is absent and Annie does not believe that the targeted group will engage in this pretended dialogue ('you stay hidden'). As the 'secondary' audience, watching the official address to this absent other, Annie feels that her doubt about the intention and efficacy of government actions is confirmed.

Yasmin: And so if it's not going to work, why do you think they did it?

Annie: Because they wanted it to work, they want it to work, because we've just explained to you, we're overloaded with illegal immigrants, not anybody in the government or anyone I spoke to can tell us how many illegal immigrants are here, how many have gone back, so that is just, well, it's playing lip service and yet this is what annoys me, you'll get our Home Office people going into say a Chinese shop, a Chinese takeaway shop and they're looking for people that have overstayed their welcome, overstayed their visas. They send one little Chinese man back home, because they caught him. What about 28,000 Romanian criminals in this country, they're here, they haven't sent them back, they haven't.

Chris: Or any of the terrorists.

Annie: One little Chinese man and I feel really sorry for them people, because what they're doing, they're earning a living in their little takeaways and they get sent back.

Chris: Well, they pick the easy target all the time, don't they?

Annie: Yeah.

Chris: Because then they can brag about what they've done.

Annie: Yeah, well, that to me, that is ridiculous, what you need is the wider, do the wider thing, leave them poor little devils who are not really doing any harm to us.

Chris: I think this was probably done as something to make people think oh look how brilliant we are and what we're actually doing, but it's a load of rubbish, really.

(Barking Focus Group, conducted by Yasmin)

Once again the conversation positions speakers as a knowing audience who are not susceptible to the somewhat foolish performances of government. More than this, the interchange reveals a more nuanced narrative around immigration, one where ineffectual government picks the 'easy target' but does not know how many people are here illegally and chooses to ignore 'the terrorists' and '28,000 Romanian criminals' (see Chapter 5). In this instance, and despite the underlying discomfort with the impact of immigration, this group viewed the Go Home van campaign as disingenuous and not in good faith. As a demonstration of this, the discussion circles back to local knowledges in a lovely, almost Pinteresque exchange:

Yasmin: But did you see it [the Go Home van] at all because it went through Barking and Dagenham, didn't it?

Chris: Well, apparently it did.

Annie: What this?

Yasmin: Yes.

Chris: But you can't go through the high street, because it's pedestrian, so I don't know where it would have gone.

(Barking Focus Group, conducted by Yasmin)

The framework through which the potential efficacy of government campaigns is judged returns to these most basic constraints of local architecture. The 'targeting' of localities reveals the distance from what is local here. The spaces where such displays might have made sense as theatre, if nothing else, are pedestrianised, 'so I don't know where it would have gone'. The claim of coming to localities, a key aspect of the theatricality of this particular initiative, is called into question. Where would it have gone and, it is implied, who would have seen it?

Without an audience, there is no political performance at all.

The suggestion of violence

> Insaaf: This picture already made me sick because I've been in the same situation that they have been in and I know what it makes, it makes you feel.
>
> (Coventry Focus Group, conducted by Kirsten)

This was the immediate response to the tweeted image of an immigration raid from one focus group participant who had been caught up in the cycle of raid–detention–release. Whereas some participants experienced Home Office campaigns as a belated but bungled recognition of their locality, others immediately placed the campaigns in a wider circulation of mediatised communications. For those who have had direct experience of raids and of detention, the trigger image of the deportation called up an array of fears and humiliations. To this constituency it was all too apparent that these circulated images and phrases were warning of the physical coercion not far behind. Jawad in Coventry explained, 'they think it might force you without ... We don't know what is going on but they're dragging like in the force, so you don't know what is going on, there is no human rights.'

Another person in the same group described their own experience:

> Insaaf: I was in the same situation. I have been detained without a reason now they took me to the Pakistani high commission, Parliament, in front of everybody they put me in handcuffs and when they took me inside the Pakistan Parliament but I saw me, they said why have they brought you here, I said I don't know ... When they check my case they say oh we are sorry, we made a mistake. They took me in front of everyone like I'm a criminal, they put handcuffs. So then they are saying we are sorry, we did a mistake, so I was very embarrassed and the whole ... In front of the whole ... I was like ... I was very embarrassed you know ... I was very embarrassed from inside for the first time in my life and very pent up.
>
> (Coventry Focus Group, conducted by Kirsten)

This personal testimony points again to the central role of humiliation in such displays: even when the exercise of authority is mistaken
('oh we are sorry, we made a mistake'), the processes of public
shaming remain. As other chapters discuss, those subject to border
enforcement were painfully conscious of the many techniques being
deployed to link migration and criminality in popular discourse
and imagination and also, increasingly, in the practices of law enforcement as described in the debates around 'crimmigration' (Stumpf,
2006, 2013).

What those who had been subjected to such processes understood
from the tweeted images of a raid is that such actions were taken to
confirm that an uncertain immigration status rendered you constantly
vulnerable to state violence and public humiliation – and also that the
state undertook actions to demonstrate this constant vulnerability to
the wider population, even when no enforcement objective was likely
to be achieved.

Although these discussion groups included people who had experienced the indignities of detention and attempted deportation, scepticism was also expressed in relation to the performative aspect of the
tweeted photographs:

> Ajala: I just want to say that I think they put this photo in Twitter
> on purpose to show the public or the local people that they are
> doing their job, they are catching people and they deporting them
> back. It's just using ... they are using this image to get ... For a
> political reason, to get more voice to work for them, you know
> what I mean. This asylum thing in the UK is not a matter of
> human rights or rights yet, it's a political matter.
> (Coventry Focus Group, conducted by Kirsten)

This view that such displays on the part of the Home Office revealed
an attention to political interest above anything else was expressed by
a number of respondents, both those seeking refuge and those who
opposed immigration. Another Coventry respondent who had been
subject to border enforcement explained in some detail how the circulation of images of border control was designed to infiltrate popular
consciousness and elicit support without the articulation of an argument or presentation of evidence:

> Femi: We are a victim of a political matter between the political
> groups in this country, that's why they put this photo on Twitter,
> to show the public they are doing better than the others of
> sending people away, whatever these people, this guy may be a

victim. Maybe his life really endangering in his country, they don't care, they just … for them he is a figure, a number, in the end of the year they want to show the public X number, we deported X number. They don't care, this X number, who they are and what has happened to them when they've been deported. So I think they put this one in purpose to show the public that they are deporting people.

(Coventry Focus Group, conducted by Kirsten)

Femi makes explicit the impact of different governmental discourses on how people are treated, in particular highlighting the wilful dehumanisation that comes with reducing people to 'X number'. In the next chapter we discuss the tactical presentation of statistical data by government. Here it is enough to note that those who have experienced the intimidation of immigration enforcement understand that the spectacular display of one raid is designed to enhance the credibility of statistical claims about immigration control.

Rupturing political space

The Go Home vans presented an unexpected intervention into public space and in public debate. First of all, the direct address to those unspoken presences of the undocumented (or 'banned' (Agamben, 1998)) created a new dynamic and theatre of immigration control. The public address through the streets revealed what had been previously avoided or brushed over: that, when we speak of 'illegals' and the enforcement of the border, these unwanted others are already among us. The geographer Eric Swyngedouw (2011) summarises a range of debates about the 'postpolitical' and the apparent closing of contemporary political space by suggesting that we live in a time when there is a push to empty political space of divergent voices and 'unrecognised' actors. He goes on to suggest that the concepts of 'the postpolitical' and 'post-democratisation' describe the process by which politics becomes increasingly closed through an assumption or imposition of consensus in the name of management. Antagonistic interest cannot be voiced or even made visible. Against this tendency, Swyngedouw argues that the struggles of those who are undocumented may represent an example of the reinsertion of the political into public space:

Those un(ac)counted in the instituted order became the stand-in for the universality of 'the People'. Today's undocumented immigrants, claiming inclusion, are a contemporary example of the political paradox, i.e., the promise of equality that is disavowed in the policing, categorization and naming of some as outside the symbolic order of the Law.

(Swyngedouw, 2011: 5)

This claim is based around the idea that the managerial politics of neoliberalism disallow some people from the status of political actor. The allowable space of political debate renders them both silent and invisible. The forced incursion into public space in order to undo this invisibility is described as the mark of the political and it is this moment of rebellion or disruption that interests Swyngedouw. What he seeks to describe are the events that reinsert politics into spaces that have been actively depoliticised. Yet in our research it is the state that disrupts the calm of existing political arrangements.

The Operation Vaken initiative and the Go Home vans seem to change the dynamic of political theatre altogether. There is an odd, almost cartoonish, ineptitude about them. Whereas other debates have indicated a falling away from participation in mainstream politics and alongside this an increasing scepticism towards what the government says and does, the Go Home vans appeared to be an attempt to somehow take the battle back to the street. If the public had ceased to believe in the actions of the political class then the Go Home vans appeared to be an attempt to change this through shifting the dynamic and location of political space. However, in the process, state enunciations appear to address the 'banned', those subject to immigration control and positioned as outside the realm of politics. Although this tactic amplifies terror for those who have experienced the physical coercion of immigration control, for other audiences this is a theatricalised interchange that further destabilises the pretence of sovereign authority. The address to the 'banned' reveals the limit of government authority and, unexpectedly, repoliticises the space of supposedly consensual community. The rest of this volume goes on to discuss the implications and impact of this disruption in different settings.

References

Agamben, G. (1998) *Homo Sacer: Sovereign Power and Bare Life*, Stanford: Stanford University Press.
Agamben, G. (1999) *Remnants of Auschwitz: The Witness and the Archive*, New York: Zone Books.

Agamben, G. (2005) *State of Exception*, Chicago and London: University of Chicago Press.

Ahmed, S. (2010) *The Promise of Happiness*, Durham and London: Duke University Press.

Austin, J.L. (1975/1962) *How to Do Things with Words, 2nd revised edition*, Cambridge, MA: Harvard University Press.

BBC (2013) 'Farage attacks "nasty" immigration posters', *BBC News*, 25 July, www.bbc.co.uk/news/uk-politics-23450438 [last accessed 21 May 2016].

BNP (2010) *Democracy, Freedom, Culture and Identity: British National Party General Elections Manifesto 2010*, Welshpool: BNP, https://web.archive.org/web/20140329093554/http://communications.bnp.org.uk/ge2010manifesto.pdf [last accessed 21 May 2016].

Bunyan, T. (1985) 'From Saltley to Orgreave via Brixton', *Journal of Law and Society*, 12 (3): 293–303.

Burnham, P. (2002) 'Labour and the politics of depoliticisation', *The British Journal of Politics and International Relations*, 3 (2): 127–49.

Butler, J. (1997) *Excitable Speech: A Politics of the Performative*, New York: Routledge.

Hay, C. (2007) *Why We Hate Politics*, Cambridge: Polity Press.

Merrick, J. (2013) 'Nick Clegg not involved in the "go home" campaign: How the "racist van" is a way to win votes', *The Independent: Voices*, 30 July, www.independent.co.uk/voices/comment/nick-clegg-not-involved-in-the-the-go-home-campaign-how-the-racist-van-is-a-way-to-win-votes-8738510.html [last accessed 21 May 2016].

Rai, S. (2015) 'Political performance: A framework for analysing democratic politics', *Political Studies*, 63 (5): 1179–97.

Saunders, C. (2014) 'Anti-politics in action? Measurement dilemmas in the study of unconventional political participation', *Political Research Quarterly*, 67 (3): 574–88.

Schedler A. (ed.) (1997) *The End of Politics? Explorations into Modern Antipolitics*, New York: Macmillan.

Stumpf, J. (2006) 'The crimmigration crisis: Immigrants, crime, and sovereign power', *American University Law Review*, 56: 367.

Stumpf, J. (2013) 'The process is the punishment in crimmigration law', in K. F. Aas and M. Bosworth (eds), *The Borders of Punishment: Criminal Justice, Citizenship and Social Exclusion*, Oxford: Oxford University Press, pp. 58–75.

Swyngedouw, E (2011) 'Interrogating post-democratization: Reclaiming egalitarian political spaces', *Political Geography*, 30 (7): 370–80.

Vaughan-Williams, N. (2009) 'The generalised bio-political border? Reconceptualising the limits of sovereign power', *Review of International Studies*, 35 (4):729–49.

Wigmore, T. (2013) 'Here's how the Tories want to stop UKIP. And it's not pretty', *The Telegraph: Blogs*, 25 July, http://blogs.telegraph.co.uk/

news/timwigmore/100228087/heres-how-the-tories-want-to-stop-ukip-and-its-not-pretty/.

Yuval-Davis, N., Wemyss, G. and Cassidy, K. (2016) 'Changing the racialized "common sense" of everyday bordering', *Open Democracy*, 17 February, www.opendemocracy.net/uk/nira-yuval-davis-georgie-wemyss-kathryn-cassidy/changing-racialized-common-sense-of-everyday-bord [last accessed 20 May 2016].

Living Research Two:
Emotions and research

Operation Vaken's posters, newspaper adverts, immigration surgeries and mobile billboards were a dramatic display, designed to reassure some citizens that the government was 'getting tough' on irregular immigration. However, the campaign also increased worries and anxiety. The survey carried out for us by Ipsos MORI of a nationally representative sample of 2,424 people (for further details see the Appendix) found that the advertising vans that drove around London in 2013 stating 'In the UK illegally? Go Home or Face Arrest' made 15 per cent of the people who were aware of them 'concerned that irregular/illegal immigration might be more widespread than they had realised'.[1] That Vaken may have distorted perceptions and feelings about the problem of irregular immigration was also a point made by Rita Chadha, Chief Executive of the Refugee and Migrant Forum of Essex and London (one of our community partners in the research). Chadha was quoted in a local newspaper in August 2013, saying that Vaken 'incites racial hatred and … inflames community tension. It's just going to scare people to think that immigration is a huge problem when it's not' (*Ilford Recorder*, 2013).

The inciting of feelings and emotions is a crucial part of immigration campaigns, yet is challenging to research. How might we identify, track and convey multisensory experiences of fear, anxiety, sadness, shock, anger, shame, disgust? How do such emotions circulate, intensify, linger and change? To what extent do social media – the content of what people post using different platforms – convey these experiences? And what about atmospheres and flows of feeling – how the sight of an immigration raid or the words 'Go Home' can

---

[1] 92 people of 603 (weighted base 627) who were aware of the Go Home vans.

elicit panicky feelings, or make some of us feel unsafe? And then there are the feelings of researchers and how these can have an impact on fieldwork, the analysis of data and ethical relationships (see Living Research Four).

Because feelings can be unconscious and are difficult to express in words, the risk is that research can end up flattening out experience. An interview transcript, for example, will have inevitably lost bodily expression and vocal nuance. This is why some researchers work between an audio/visual recording and a transcript. Listening to or watching an interview or research interaction can enrich analysis, helping us to notice extra-linguistic data – when someone is being sarcastic or feels uncomfortable. This type of work is also more time-consuming, so needs to be addressed in the planning stages of a study. Dissemination is another point in research where it is possible to reanimate data with some of its emotions and sensuality. As our project developed, we began to experiment with methods of conveying the emotional and embodied aspects of experiences of immigration control by using film and dramatisations of fieldwork scenes (practices that are discussed in the growing literature on 'performative social science', see FQS, 2008).

Although all research is emotional and sensual, immigration is a subject that arouses strong feelings across social and political divides, bringing with it particular methodological and ethical challenges. It is what methodologists sometimes call a 'sensitive topic', meaning that it can feel threatening to both research participants and researchers. Among the challenges of researching sensitive topics, Julie Brannen (1988), drawing from the ideas of the sociologist Erving Goffman, has identified the increased risks of sanctions and stigma for those participating in such research. In addition, she suggests:

> respondents are likely to find confronting and telling their stories a stressful experience. This is a problem for researchers as well as respondents. The researcher therefore has some responsibility for protecting the respondent. Protection is required both with respect to the confidences disclosed and the emotions which may be aroused and expressed.
>
> (pp. 552–3)

Building relationships with research participants over time, demonstrating knowledge about the politics of an issue and carefully anonymising data are all ways of 'desensitising' and 'dejeopardising' qualitative research (see Lee, 1993). For example, the policy-makers whom Will interviewed (see Chapter 3) felt uncomfortable when talking about the government's approach to immigration as they are expected to be neutral implementers of policy. One way of reducing the threat of the interviews was not to record them. In quantitative surveys, thought needs to be given to the format of questions, the order in which they are placed and how they are contextualised (see Bhattacharyya, 2015).

But is it unrealistic or even patronising to think that we can shield individuals from the emotionality of a topic such as immigration? And how ethical is it for us to treat difficult emotions and experiences as data? The latter point was an issue that came up in one of our focus groups with asylum seekers and refugees, facilitated by Kirsten. During the focus group, a young woman began to talk about the existential insecurity of being an asylum seeker, of feeling that she was wasting her life. She was unable to plan for a future, unable to study. She felt as if she was waiting in limbo while the Home Office made a decision about her immigration status. Overcome in telling us her story, she broke down in tears.

Kirsten, herself a minoritised and migrant woman, did not record this part of the conversation (another participant in the focus group had asked her to turn off the audio recording). Kirsten's fieldwork notes describe how she and the group rallied around the young woman, trying to reassure and comfort her (the group had been meeting for three months, so people knew each other relatively well). In this case, Kirsten's response went beyond that of the 'empathic witness' (Kleinman, 1988) and had practical consequences: audio data were lost from the recording and the time given to comforting the young woman also meant that the focus group was cut short; there was less time for others to speak, resulting in a partial and shorter interview. For Kamala Visweswaran (1994) such redacted accounts are full of vital information. They can force us to feel and hopefully investigate further how historical and institutional contexts can affect the micro-interactions and ethical relationships produced by a project. For Riessman (2005: 473), 'The investigator's emotions are highly relevant to conversations about ethics because emotions do moral work: they embody judgments about value'.

Although we can never know in advance how emotions might play out in a study, we had anticipated that the focus group interviews could be upsetting for some people and this was where our community partnerships were important. The local organisations that we each worked with set up our interviews and were able to provide initial support to research participants and, if necessary, refer them to other local services for more specialist help. In practice this never happened (as far as we are aware). None the less, we need to think more critically about the ethical and political implications of this outsourcing of emotional support in the aftermath of research, especially when partnership working is increasingly valued by funders. Did we leave trails of damage behind us with consequences for others?

Looking back on the project and thinking about what we might have done differently, it feels as if we should have talked more about how we would respond to the emotions and feelings that are evoked by and which surround immigration campaigns and that become a part of research. We should also have talked to one another about our assumptions and ideas about what emotions and feelings *are*. The latter point is especially important because it impacts upon the methods that are chosen for a project and how we interpret research data. For instance, if we recognise that research participants and researchers are 'defended subjects' (Hollway and Jefferson, 2013), whose own biographies and feelings of anxiety can affect what is said and/or observed, then more complex forms of reporting and interpreting data are needed, which do not valorise what is said as a source of access to a true self (Atkinson, 1997). This might include providing contextual description before using interview extracts to give a sense of where an extract is situated within a wider interaction, social context or biography and why there might be layers of meaning underneath what is superficially meant. It can also include the iterative analysis of interview extracts with fieldwork notes, identifying areas of tension and/or contradiction between and within accounts.

In hindsight it is apparent that as a team we took different approaches to emotions, which had an impact on our observations, interviews and basic recording practices. For instance, some of our fieldnotes are rich in description about localities and research interactions. They are more varied in the attention given to our own feelings and how we might make sense of these within the wider project, as individuals and as providing insight into our varying social differences, research roles, the differential distribution of emotional labour within the research team and how these might all impact on partnership working. As always the work of research and the thinking and feeling that goes with it extends far beyond the funding of a study. Even the publication of this book does not bring it to a close.

In interviews on 'sensitive topics' emotions can be both intensely felt and closer to the surface of research relationships. There are several issues to think about in research where topic threat is prevalent:

1 What recording practices (such as audio/visual recording of interviews or events) might you adopt to lessen the threat of a topic? What consequences might these different practices have for the data?
2 What are your ethical responsibilities as a researcher when individual/s become distressed because of what is triggered for them by the subjects that are raised by the research?
3 What about the researcher? Can you think of any ways in which a researcher's feelings can be taken account of in study? What support might be possible?

References

Atkinson, P. (1997) 'Narrative turn or blind alley?', *Qualitative Health Research*, 7 (3): 325–44.

Bhattacharyya, G. (2015) 'Immigration control, racism and public opinion', *Mapping Immigration Controversy blog*, 7 January, https://mappingimmigrationcontroversy.com/2015/01/07/290/ [accessed 1 March 2016].

Brannen, J. (1988) 'The study of sensitive subjects', *Sociological Review*, 36 (3): 552–63.

FQS (2008) Performative Social Science. *Special Issue*, 9 (2), www.qualitative-research.net/index.php/fqs/issue/view/10 [accessed 2 March 2016].

Hollway, W. and Jefferson, T. (2013) *Doing Qualitative Research Differently: Free Association, Narrative and the Interview Method*, 2nd ed., London: Sage.

Ilford Recorder (2013) '"Go home or face arrest" van driving around Redbridge is a "political stunt"', 2 August, www.ilfordrecorder.co.uk/news/politics/go_home_or_face_arrest_van_driving_around_redbridge_is_a_political_stunt_1_2313424 [accessed 1 March 2016].

Kleinman, A. (1988) *The Illness Narratives: Suffering, Healing and the Human Condition*, New York: Basic Books.

Lee, R. (1993) *Doing Research on Sensitive Topics*, London: Sage.

Riessman, C. (2005) 'Exporting ethics: A narrative about narrative research in South India', *Health*, 9 (4): 473–90.

Visweswaran, K. (1994) *Fictions of Feminist Ethnography*, Minneapolis, MN: University of Minnesota Press.

3

Immigration and the limits of statistical government

Camden Town Hall in North London is a popular venue for weddings and civil ceremonies. In November 2013 it was the venue for the marriage of a Miao Guo, a Chinese national in her twenties and Massimo Ciabattini, an Italian man in his thirties, for which elaborate preparations had been made, including a post-service reception and a hotel room for the night. The ceremony was dramatically interrupted by Home Office Immigration Enforcement officers wearing flak jackets and accompanied, oddly enough, by journalists.

The couple were pulled apart and taken into separate rooms for questioning. Bridesmaids were also interviewed. This happened because of a tip-off from the registrar, who suspected the marriage was a sham (being undertaken to get a visa), after observing that the couple had had trouble spelling each other's names. Half an hour of questioning later, and with abundant evidence that the marriage was not a sham, the government officials left and the ceremony was restarted (Hutton, 2013; Weaver, 2013). A Home Office spokesman was reported to comment at the time of this failed raid, 'it is either the best sham wedding I have ever seen or it is real' (Hutton, 2013).

Journalists had been invited to the raid in the hope that they could write about UK immigration control in a more impressive light than the one that transpired. 'Performance politics', as discussed in the previous chapter, requires the state to put on convincing public displays that the 'audience' finds compelling. The performance of the border as a space of fear and potential violence has to infiltrate the public sphere, in this case with the help of the local media.

While the performance politics of raids work to spread fear, this incident also reminds us of the fragility, or even the stupidity, of contemporary immigration policy. Where policy is operating primarily at the level of affect, psychological manipulation and appearances, there is always the potential for this to blow back at those with power. Making things seem 'real' is an ongoing challenge, especially for the

Home Office because – in a way which no other Whitehall department faces to the same extent – media attention to immigration is relentless and highly charged politically. As we learnt through our interviews, virtually everything the Home Office does must be considered with audience reaction in mind, shaping its policy-making and implementation processes.

Developing the insights into performative politics drawn from Shirin Rai's (2015) work in Chapter 2, here we seek to understand government immigration campaigns in terms of the logics, rationalities and anxieties that underpin them. We will do this by exploring the techniques of government used in Operation Vaken through an engagement with, and extension of, the terms circulating in policy circles themselves, framed through questions of liberalism, neoliberalism, postliberalism and preliberalism. In doing so, we pull out some of the contradictions demonstrated in the previous chapter whereby tools of persuasion and enforcement rely each on the other. The analysis in this chapter is informed by a number of discussions and interviews with policy-makers and advisers, many of which were necessarily off the record. These included current Home Office and former Home Office officials, and also civil servants from elsewhere in Whitehall, including the Department of Business, Innovation and Skills (BIS) and the Treasury.

In summary, in this chapter we discuss government migration campaigns in terms of the policy logic that shapes them. Specifically, we argue:

1   Liberal government treats issues like migration in the aggregate, meaning that statistics and macroeconomics tend to be the ultimate arbiters of 'good' policy.
2   This emphasis on aggregates has lost legitimacy where migration is concerned, meaning that the politics and policy of migration is increasingly dominated by affective, symbolic and mediated issues.
3   In place of liberal government, a distinctive style of policy and politics has emerged in the Home Office, that is an elaborate and occasionally threatening form of reputation management.

Liberalism via quantification

> We have the chance in this century to achieve an open world, an open economy, and an open global society with unprecedented opportunities for people and business.
>
> (Tony Blair, speech to the World Economic Forum at Davos, 2000)

Migration is likely to enhance economic growth and the welfare of both natives and migrants ... There is little evidence that native workers are harmed by immigration ... The broader fiscal impact of migration is likely to be positive.

(Cabinet Office, 2001: 5–7)

In terms of the politics of migration, the above quotes seem to come from a very different political era to the one in which we write. The proportion of the British public mentioning 'immigration' as one of the most important issues facing Britain was under 10 per cent in 2000, but had risen to over 40 per cent only eight years later (Duffy and Frere-Smith, 2014). The case for greater migration at this time was both normative and utilitarian: people *should* be allowed to live where they choose, and moreover this will bring *benefits* in terms of levels of wealth and quality of life overall. Within a decade, this sort of rhetoric had disappeared from mainstream policy discourse. But in order to understand the rationalities (and irrationalities) of contemporary government of migration, we need to consider how the normative and utilitarian argument for freedom of movement has functioned until relatively recently.

In a lecture series given at the Collège de France in 1977–78, the French philosopher Michel Foucault identified two parallel forms of political power that together constitute the modern state (Foucault, 2007). Firstly, there is the 'perspective' that Foucault defines as 'sovereignty', which aims at securing the borders and interior of a given territory. The chief purpose of a sovereign is to keep things as they are, that is, to continue to be respected as the sovereign within borders that do not shift. This conceptualisation was present in the sixteenth-century English philosopher Thomas Hobbes's classical vision of the modern state. For Hobbes, sovereign power is centralised and sufficiently potent that it can oblige obedience from all of its 'subjects'. As Foucault explains, 'the end of sovereignty is circular; it refers back to the exercise of sovereignty. The good is obedience to the law, so that the good proposed by sovereignty is that people obey it' (Foucault, 2007: 98). Securing borders, enforcing law and defeating enemies are the key tasks of a sovereign.

Secondly, there is the 'perspective' of 'government'. Where sovereignty is focused on applying given laws within a particular territory, government looks at how to facilitate and encourage certain *dynamics within a population*. This is a very different way of conceiving of politics:

Population no longer appears as a collection of subjects of right, as a collection of subject wills who must obey the sovereign's will through the intermediary regulations, laws, edicts and so on. It will be considered as a set of processes to be managed at the level and on the basis of what is natural in these processes.

(Foucault, 2007:70)

The 'processes' in question are effects of individual behaviour and choices, scaled up to the level of the population as a whole. Births, deaths, marriage, sickness, productivity, income, assets and so on are aspects of the population that government is concerned to improve – or at least, not to damage. To this list, we might add migration, as it can affect the size of a population.

Over the eighteenth century, this form of power became predominant in European states, producing a new form of administrative government able to act on population in an expert and measured fashion. To do this, new forms of quantitative knowledge were required, capable of representing population dynamics. In particular, Foucault points to the rise of political economy in the late eighteenth century, focused on markets but also on other 'natural' dynamics influencing population such as agricultural production and birth rates. No less importantly, statistics offered a basis on which to represent things *in the aggregate*, so that trends and empirical laws could emerge amongst events that otherwise would seem contingent, accidental or moral and political in nature. In this way, the statistical gaze takes normative questions of individual conduct or indeed chance, and scales them up until they are empirical questions of population dynamics.

This statistical view of society is simultaneously liberal and scientific: its liberalism is entrenched in its methodology. There are various ways in which we can understand this synthesis of quantitative social science and liberalism. Firstly, modern statistics assumes that aggregate processes are the result of diverse individual decisions, preferences and judgements. As Foucault puts it, the one thing that government assumes is common to all people is 'desire'. Thus, the driving force behind migration flows, for instance, is assumed to be freely taken *choices* to seek work, better quality of life, family reunification, education or whatever else. The governmental perspective on a problem such as migration would involve seeking to alter the value of these different goals, so as to influence the aggregate dynamics in certain ways.

Secondly, statistics have a liberal quality because they aim to take *everyone* into account. In the search for the normal or average individual, statisticians were also seeking a way of representing society *as a whole*. The governmental emphasis on the aggregate is a tacit form of collectivism that potentially allows individual conduct to be judged in terms of how it effects net outcomes, rather than on the basis of any political, moral or cultural value or prejudice.

Thirdly, statistics *potentially* have a cultural blindness about them, at least on some questions. All quantitative methodologies involve some assumption of equivalence (Desrosières, 1998), through which multiple and separate cases can be treated in the same way. Where differences are being represented, they are represented on the basis of some principle of potential sameness. So, in order to say that 'he is 20 per cent taller than her', there must be a shared idea called 'height' and a shared understanding of proportions.

What has become known as 'evidence-based policy-making' or doing 'What Works' is an effort to promote a dispassionate, scientific perspective within government. The utilitarian statistical ethos *can* serve as a way of keeping unwelcome cultural and political questions at bay, bracketing issues of 'policy' as if separate from those of 'politics'. France, for example, famously leaves out questions of ethnicity from its national statistics data, ostensibly on the basis that ethnicity does not affect the status of French nationals as citizens. But this omission makes it harder to speak authoritatively about the extent of racism in French society. In a more technocratic spirit, emphasising economic growth as the ultimate indicator of progress allows an issue like migration to be culturally and politically diffused (as New Labour sought to do), and each new arrival into the country can be viewed simply as another anonymous contributor to aggregate output. Economics is potentially the most effective tool for depoliticisation of an issue. For instance, representing an issue as a matter of expertise, economic evidence and *policy* is a way of keeping it separate from matters of identity, ethnicity and *politics*. Viewing it from the perspective of *government* can be a way of avoiding the perspective of *sovereignty*. For various reasons, this strategy no longer seems to work in the British context. Before we explore this failure further, we need to consider two alternative rationalities of power that represent a departure from statistical liberalism.

Rationalities of disaggregation

As the sociologist and statistician Alain Desrosières (1998) has highlighted, the statistical focus on population aggregates depends for its legitimacy on some universalist, quasi-democratic idea of 'society', in which we all have a stake. Yet it is precisely a sense of the social aggregate that has been gradually dismantled as an object of government since the 1970s (Rose, 1996b). While it was possible for New Labour to use GDP as a justification for migration in the early 2000s, it is telling that public anxiety about migration rose long before the recession, which began in early 2008. Aggregate welfare does not count for much when individuals are concerned about their own personal welfare, and view immigration as a direct threat to it.

What happens if statistical government is no longer adequate for purposes of administrative decision-making? Two alternative forms of rationality are worth noting: neoliberalism, and 'postliberalism' as it has been discussed in the recent British policy context. While these are mutually antagonistic in various ways, they share a tendency to disaggregate, dissociate and distinguish worthy populations from unworthy populations (see also Chapter 5). Rhetorically they are poles apart, but they have a mutual compatibility that is often overlooked, as we now explore, starting with neoliberalism.

Neoliberalism

In Foucault's account, the key difference between liberalism and neoliberalism lies in how the market is represented and idealised. Liberalism views the market as a separate space of autonomous freedom, outside of the social and political spheres; neoliberalism treats all spheres of human conduct and all human capacities as essentially economic in nature (Brown, 2015). From a neoliberal perspective, economic choices are not simply those which are exercised in the marketplace in the process of monetised exchange but *all* choices regarding how to use one's free time, who to marry, who to vote for, what to learn, and how to live. The key function of competition, from a neoliberal perspective, is that it distinguishes that which is most valuable, whether inside or outside the market. Hence, the main virtue of capitalism is its capacity to separate people out (winners from losers, leaders from followers, strivers from skivers), rather than to integrate in the way that economic liberals had celebrated since Adam Smith. For this reason, nationalism can play an important part within neoliberalism, to the extent that nations are acting like competitive units, striving to become the 'best' and to 'beat' others in the 'global race' (Davies, 2014). As the geographer David Harvey puts it, 'the neoliberal state needs nationalism of a certain sort to survive' (2005: 85).

One of the most celebrated exponents of the neoliberal worldview was the Chicago School economist Gary Becker, whose concept of 'human capital' assumed that individuals had the freedom to augment themselves, through education and other decisions, so as to increase their economic value in the marketplace (Becker, 1976). Viewing humans as items of 'capital' rather than as members of population has a disaggregating effect, which represents a departure from liberal governmentality. In the sphere of migration, it is manifest in the much-heralded 'Australian-style points system', which assesses applications for residency by adding up points earned on the basis of age, skills, qualifications and linguistic ability.

This points-based system has been much celebrated by right-wing politicians in the UK, and was adopted as the official policy of the UK Independence Party (UKIP) in the run-up to the 2015 election and the 2016 EU referendum – ignoring the fact that such a system had already been introduced by the Labour government for non-EU nationals, in effect from 2008. The curious forms of political triangulation that the 'Australian-style points system' has enabled can be seen in the then UKIP leader Nigel Farage's claim that this system is the only 'fair' one (Farage, 2015) and UKIP's defence of its 'principle of equal application to all people' (UKIP, 2015, n.p.).

The idea of a 'points-based system', rooted in calculations of human capital, has the veneer of administrative governmentality, but it conceals a more violent sovereign logic focused on inclusion and exclusion. It may even serve to entrench certain prejudices, regarding the work-rate or economic mindset of different cultural identities. Increasingly, immigration is a policy area where governmentality and sovereignty are entangled in ways that collapse arguments about economics and national identity into one another. It is worth recognising the extent to which neoliberal rationality – which extends economics into all spheres of conduct – facilitates this entanglement.

Postliberalism

The idea of 'postliberalism' emerged in UK policy discussions in the years immediately following the global financial crisis, along with the terms 'Red Tory' and 'Blue Labour'.[1] As the names indicate, this

---

[1] In the UK, red is associated with left-wing politics and the Labour Party (through residues of socialism) and blue with the right-wing Conservative (or 'Tory') Party (the opposite of these colours' political associations in the USA). 'Red Tory' refers to Conservatives with political sympathies with certain 'left-wing' values, such as social security, community and equality. 'Blue Labour' refers to Labour supporters with political sympathies with certain 'right-wing' values, such as tradition, nationalism, family and cultural homogeneity. These agendas are heavily overlapping and their protagonists are in regular dialogue with each other.

mixing up of categories was a way of transcending left/right political divisions, laying out a more socially conservative and economically localist new policy agenda (Blond, 2010; Geary and Pabst, 2015). Fuelling this new intellectual insurgency was a sense that policy orthodoxy had been set by a technocratic metropolitan elite, whose support for migration was out of step with the rest of the country (see also Chapter 6). In the words of Blue Labour 'guru' Maurice Glasman, 'on managerialism, modernity and the market, Blair ultimately served the interests of the rich and the status quo' (Riddell, 2011, n.p.). Often, the blame was deemed to lie specifically with economists:

> Freedom of movement at moderate levels, like immigration itself, is a benefit both to the movers and the country they move to. But the liberal economists and politicians who dominate the EU debate gave little thought to large-scale movement nor do they seem to have realised the extent to which they were eroding national social contracts.
>
> (Goodhart, 2014)

For the political commentator David Goodhart, who has done the most to advance the idea of 'postliberalism', opposition to immigration is an inevitable outcome of natural psychological tendencies that lead us to favour 'people like us' (Goodhart, 2014). Liberalism, for Goodhart, is ultimately a denial of human nature, just as economics is when it views people as isolated rational utility-maximisers. In its avowed localism and populism, postliberalism explicitly rejects the centralised, technocratic perspective of the statistician and the economic administrator. Part of the postliberal critique is that liberal government acts in an impersonal, generalising, calculated manner, preventing a more ethically substantive or publicly meaningful form of policy. Yet what such an alternative policy would be is *by definition* impossible to formalise as a set of rules. Glasman, for example, suggests that a much tighter immigration policy would still need to make 'exceptions' on ethical grounds, but the postliberal ethos resists systematising these (Riddell, 2011).

Despite this inconsistency, we can make out a certain resonance between the postliberal critique of economics and the psychological critique of economics, which has produced behavioural and happiness economics. Goodhart claims that postliberalism 'has a view of human nature that aims to capture people in their messy reality rather than reduce them to a single, dominant drive such as self-interest or a desire for autonomy' (2014: 1). Yet he also claims that group attachments are 'hard-wired into us' and that a preference for 'people like us' is a 'simple reality of life', suggesting that for him there are nevertheless a few dominant psychological (or biological) drives that can be isolated when developing policy. This is an example of what might be termed 'neocommunitarianism', in which psychological and biological evidence is used to help reconstruct the government of individual decision-making (Davies, 2012). The rise of 'nudging' as a way of altering individual behaviour through the redesign of 'choice architectures' is another example of this, through which everyday techniques such as 'social marketing' and food-labelling can be seen as forms of intervention (Jones et al., 2013).

A key feature of behaviourally attuned policy is that it pays far greater attention to the aesthetics and affective dimensions of governmental intervention, so that all sorts of other factors come into play, including the learnt habits, emotions, neurological substrates and social influences that condition behaviour (Dolan et al., 2010). Altering behaviour is a matter no longer simply of tweaking 'incentives' but of altering multiple aspects of the social and material environment, in much the way that advertisers have long done. As we shall explore, this heightened policy attention to emotions and behaviour related to migration is arguably a key feature of the postliberal government and 'performance politics', although the notion that experts might seek to influence individual behaviour through manipulating their environment is far from new.

Attempts to anchor advertising and management in scientific psychology date back to the 1920s (Baritz, 1960; Rose, 1996a). Governments have attempted to influence psychological indicators such as 'public opinion' and 'morale' for almost as long. But the rise of 'nudging' in the early twenty-first century represents a renewed concern with small-scale cultural and visual messaging, which bypasses the conscious mind or explicit discussion. In that sense, it shares a communicative rationality with 'dog whistle' politics, recognising that the implicit and oblique dimensions of public discourse can be more powerful than what is explicit or direct. While nudging remains a technocratic pursuit, its concern with the performative, normative and symbolic dimensions of policy interventions is in keeping with postliberal critique.

In its antipathy to elites, technocrats and orthodox economics, postliberalism is ultimately a challenge to the very idea of 'government', in Foucault's sense of an 'administration of things ... a technology of power' (Foucault, 2007: 49). It is certainly an affront to *statistical* government, which employs models and aggregates as the measure of all political action. It resists the very idea of treating all people in the same way, which it characterises as a metropolitan conceit. Yet in doing so, it inadvertently corroborates aspects of the neoliberal project of rationalised discrimination, which seeks to separate the enterprising from the non-enterprising. Both rest on a critique of the generalising aspect of liberalism, and an effort to develop policies capable of distinguishing the worthy from the unworthy migrant (see Chapter 5). Both depart from the abstractions of the free market, towards an account of underlying human drives – competitiveness for neoliberals, and cultural sameness for postliberals.

Most significantly, both neoliberalism and postliberalism signal a revival of sovereign power and a commensurate decline in liberal governmentality in Foucault's sense. Political questions of territory, nationhood, border, security and law return to the fore, overwhelming (or perhaps co-opting) questions of efficiency, macroeconomic growth, utility and aggregate welfare in the process. The need to *display* 'toughness' on immigration, to speak in terms of national symbolism (as opposed to aggregate outcomes), to sympathise with personal and local experiences of migration (as opposed to evidence of macroeconomic effects) has led to a collapse in the imagined distinction between 'policy' and 'politics', to the point where Home Office policy-makers mobilise images of state violence and far-right rhetoric in order to manage migration. We now consider how this intermingling of 'policy' and 'politics' appears from the perspective of the Home Office itself.

Rationalities of contemporary migration policy in the UK

Being able to interview civil servants is always difficult. It involves a high degree of trust, and even then gaining consent to record an interview is almost impossible. Having an informal coffee with a government official, accompanied by a notebook, is the more likely scenario. However, with migration policy, even this turns out to be a something of a stretch, such are the sensitivities, controversies and media interest in this area. The potential costs of any discussion of the topic are deemed too high to take risks.

Through a series of introductions, however, Will was able to meet with civil servants, including past and present Home Office officials, although on very strict terms. Attempts to 'snowball' these contacts (i.e. to use them to establish contacts for further interviews) had mixed results. When a mere reference was made about wanting to meet another Home Office official, for example, a terse email quickly arrived from Will's first contact, pointing out that this was a clear breach of the agreed secrecy surrounding their discussion. Employees of think tanks are understandably less paranoid, and interviews with influential immigration policy thinkers were more straightforward.

What follows, then, is a collection of impressions and reports from a series of conversations – in various coffee shops around Westminster – over the course of 2013–14. While these didn't generate 'data' in any tangible, duplicable form, they played an important part in our project, helping us to glimpse something of the problem of immigration as it appears to those in Whitehall, and the Home Office in particular. Especially for the latter, we got a strong sense of an organisation that feels embattled and misunderstood, both by the rest of Whitehall and by liberal critics. This no doubt contributed to the lack of enthusiasm for co-operating with a sociological research project.

The governing rationality of the Home Office seems to be very different from that of other Whitehall departments, and we were interested in understanding how and why this is, with a view to better understanding how a policy such as Operation Vaken becomes possible. In the terms outlined in this chapter, it would appear that various aspects of contemporary migration policy defy basic tenets of liberal government. The question is whether they might be any better understood in terms of neoliberalism or postliberalism.

One significant feature of migration as a contemporary policy issue is that efforts to treat it as 'just' a matter of policy often produce the opposite of the desired effect. Liberal techniques of depoliticisation outlined in this chapter tend to be not simply ineffective but counterproductive. Research carried out by the think tank British Future on attitudes to migration found that, when politicians or businesses discuss the economic benefits of migration to the national economy, this can produce some very negative reactions (Katwala et al., 2014). Talk of benefits to the 'national economy' in focus groups led to the response that this wasn't a benefit to *my* economy. As one of the policy-makers we interviewed remarked, 'while the Treasury might be believed on its growth figures, it will never be believed on its economic impacts of immigration'. A study conducted on belief in conspiracy theories across the UK population found that 55 per cent of people believe the statement 'UK Government is hiding the truth about the number of immigrants living here' is probably or definitely true, compared to only 25 per cent believing it is definitely or probably untrue (Faulkner Rogers, 2015).

Research on attitudes repeatedly finds a common view, that people believe that politicians and policy-makers do not know or care how migration is affecting *local* streets or *local* labour markets. British Future classed the majority of the British public as the 'anxious middle', to whom talk of the macroeconomic benefits seems untrustworthy or patronising. Efforts to ground a public debate about migration in a set of 'facts' or statistics are found to harden the position of those who are sceptical about immigration, to whom statistics are associated with the interests of politicians and elites. As British Future argues, 'People understand "the economy" through their direct experience – jobs, wages and the money in their pocket – rather than through GDP and macroeconomic statistics' (Katwala et al., 2014: 28).

Instead of focusing on statistics and economics, there is a perception that politicians and businesses need to speak a more emotional and communitarian language, focused on qualitative human experiences and anxieties. For many of the policy-makers we spoke with, this meant sympathising with the view that it's 'not racist' to want less immigration; recognising deep-set anxieties about the competence of the state to secure the border; understanding that immigration *can* cause disorientating social change at a local level, including in the labour market. To do this, political rhetoric has to switch away from utilitarian liberalism (of economics and statistics) towards the language of belonging, national identity, security and symbolism. Or in Foucault's terms, migration policy needs to be viewed from the perspective of sovereignty not of governmentality. One interviewee gave an example of a meeting chaired by the then Prime Minister David Cameron, in which someone referred to migration 'regulations', to which Cameron responded tersely – 'those aren't regulations: they're the law'. The message here is that migration cannot be treated as a purely administrative issue without inciting impassioned public responses. One way of pursuing this is to simply refuse engagement in statistical-utilitarian discussion. A written question by Labour peer Lord Beecham asked the Treasury to reveal 'the annual benefits paid to EU migrants in the UK and the contribution of those individuals to the public purse through income tax receipts and VAT', to which the answer came back in February 2016 'the information is not available' (Waugh, 2016). On the other hand, it is argued that once the qualitative, emotional and local perspective of voters has been expressed, the legitimacy of more open borders and labour markets might be restored to some extent. This was the view expressed to us by many of the policy-makers we spoke to, including in the Home Office. Subsequent political developments, particularly debates and developments around the UK's June 2016 referendum on whether to remain a member of the EU, do not appear to have borne out this latter argument.

The qualitative, affective impact that the state seeks above all others is an image of being 'tough' at the border. We were told that private polling had been carried out by the Home Office under the Labour Home Secretary John Reid in the mid-2000s, which found that the public was more trusting of uniformed border agency staff (who are perceived as characteristically 'tough') than of politicians (who are perceived as characteristically liberal and metropolitan). Following this, a rebranding of the UK borders was undertaken in 2006, so as to amplify the sense of a national border, via flags, insignia, uniforms and other symbols (see also Chapters 1 and 2). Meanwhile, a communications strategy aimed at getting more images of immigration raids into the media was launched as early as 2006, long before the Home Office's social-media-based campaigns of 2013. This included inviting journalists along to witness raids, so as to divert media attention to the physical 'toughness' of the border, and away from the rhetoric and perceived elitism of politicians. Ultimately, the very fact that vans displaying the message 'Go Home' were ever driven around Britain's streets at all needs to be understood in the context of this perceived need for the state to *seem* tough in the eyes of the voting public. Of course, this ignores the fear that such messages inculcate amongst various marginalised populations, as we will discuss in subsequent chapters.

A second significant feature of migration as a policy issue is that it has a very high media profile, meaning that the Home Office often tends to develop new policy and respond to policy failures at an unusually high speed. While some interviewees suggested that keeping migration out of the news altogether was the ideal political scenario for the Home Secretary, the medium-term implausibility of this means that any Home Office needs to pay constant attention to the news cycle. We were unable to discover precisely how the Go Home vans and accompanying Twitter campaign had been conceived, but most interviewees took the view that it had likely been an ill-thought-out effort within the Home Office communications team to win positive headlines amongst the anti-migration media. Interviewees suggested that being perceived as illiberal in the media (or upsetting the liberal media) is something the Home Office communications team is generally pleased with. On the other hand, given deep levels of mistrust in the government's ability to manage immigration, even very tough messaging can backfire if it reminds the public of issues (such as illegal immigration) that have otherwise fallen out of the news cycle.

Coupled with the challenges that come with immigration having such a high media profile is a recognition that, since the early years of the twenty-first century, migration has become one of the top two issues (and often the top one) that concern the voting public, according to polls (Duffy and Frere-Smith, 2014). Some of those interviewed by Will argued that this places the Home Office in a very different position from other, more technocratic, less popularly controversial Whitehall departments. This context means that policy 'success' and 'failure' are something other than mere technical efficacy or efficiency. Policies need to *look* effective, as much as be effective, something which other Whitehall departments do not necessarily understand. As one policy-maker put it:

> its sheer salience is also important ... an approach which says 'let's insulate rational policy from public politics' just isn't viable with this level of salience.
>
> (Policy interview, conducted by Will)

Others suggested to us that the awareness of depth of public feeling on the topic pervaded the Home Office, influencing migration policy development at every step. This emerged also in our negotiations with the survey company on the wording of some of the questions in the survey we commissioned, where there was nervousness about asking questions which might produce critical findings about the Home Office as one of its major clients (see Living Research Six).

The Home Office's own stated rationality for the Go Home vans was an economic one, as set out in their published evaluation (Home Office, 2013). Voluntary repatriations of 'illegal immigrants' cost the government on average £1,000 per person, while enforced ones cost £15,000, so encouraging those 'in the UK illegally' to 'go home' has apparent fiscal justification. The Home Office official we spoke to explained that the policy of helping 'illegal immigrants' to leave the country is actually a 'generous' one, in that their airfare is paid for by the taxpayer. While the vans alluded to 'free advice and help with travel documents', they made no mention of the free airfare, which our Home Office interviewee explained was necessary to avoid antagonising the tabloid press. From the Home Office's perspective, the position of the media makes this an impossible situation, in that the British state is unable to publicise the full 'help' it is actually providing people to 'go home', for fear that this would seem like a free handout to the undeserving. In other words, the messaging of 'Go Home or face arrest' came out of an effort to increase voluntary repatriation, while continuing to appear 'tough' on illegal immigration. There is little consideration here for whether this, or the posters stating 'Is life here hard? Going home is simple', 'This plane can take

you home, we can book your tickets' displayed in immigration reporting centres to asylum applicants might be viewed as threatening,
rather than generous, by those seeking refuge from dangerous 'home'
countries. As one of the speakers at a research event we held in
Glasgow, a member of the 'Glasgow Girls' (see Chapter 4) who had
gone through the asylum system herself and continued to campaign
on migrants' rights issues, said:

> I mean, having little planes hanging from the ceiling, you know,
> these are people who are seeking sanctuary and you're basically
> telling them, 'Life in the UK's difficult, going home is simple.' It's
> not simple. You know, I would love to see them trying, go to some
> of these countries and see how long they would last in it.
> (Amal Azzudin, speaking at MIC policy briefing in Glasgow,
> April 2014)

The emotional responses of those who were ostensibly targeted by
the posters offering voluntary removal appeared less important to
the Home Office than the economic efficiency of the campaign,
however. The formal evaluation of the Go Home vans suggested that
they represented a cost saving to the taxpayer. The campaign cost
only £9,740, but was deemed responsible for sixty voluntary repatriations. According to the Operation Vaken evaluation, removal of
these sixty people could otherwise have cost up to £830,000 in
enforced departures or up to £260,000 a year in costs to public
services (Home Office, 2013). A different question is whether they
were also deemed a public communications success. It seemed as if
the level of publicity that the vans attracted was never predicted, and
there was anger expressed in various media outlets and by senior
politicians.

The fact that the campaign was not repeated, despite the alleged
fiscal benefit, would suggest that it was not judged as a political
success overall (see Chapter 1 for discussion of the challenges to the
campaign by RAMFEL and those who complained to the Advertising
Standards Authority). However, the publicity – which coincided with
the Twitter campaign of raids being photographed – may be assumed
to have had some 'dog whistle' benefits, from the perspective of communication strategists seeking to appease the anti-immigration sections of the public. The extent of this 'secondary' messaging – and
ways it may have backfired, such as increasing anxiety that immigration is a severe enough problem to require such tough measures – was
explored in our research and these findings are discussed in subsequent chapters.

The exceptional status of immigration, as an issue that defies reduction to the status of an economic or statistical matter, needs to be seen in the context of the Home Office's own exceptional status. The ministry has been frequently mired in controversies and media attacks, leading it to be represented as a 'political graveyard' (Painter, 2008). The Home Office is responsible for areas of policy that are especially enticing from the perspective of the tabloid press: policing, prisons, terrorism, asylum, drugs, antisocial behaviour, all in addition to migration. This means that the department as a whole operates on a relentless communications cycle, which inculcates a sense of paranoia and watching one's back. In addition to this, there are deep structural reasons why the Home Office encounters regular conflicts with other Whitehall departments, especially where the latter operate according to more liberal economic rationalities. For these reasons, one interviewee joked that the internal philosophy of the Home Office could be summed up by the well-known chant of Millwall football fans, 'No one likes us, we don't care'.

Neoliberalism with a postliberal face

The celebratory rhetoric of 'globalisation' that characterised the early New Labour years may have been largely a reiteration of government commitments to 'business' and market 'flexibility', but it had one political advantage as well. It offered a language with which elites could speak publicly about the political economy that they subscribed to, namely one based around market liberalism. From this perspective, as we have discussed, migration represents a net benefit in the aggregate, because it increases labour market efficiency and represents a positive contribution to the macroeconomy. Lurking within this ideology is the potential for a more discriminatory neoliberal perspective, which distinguishes between different migrants in terms of their human capital or capacity for innovation or likely balance of fiscal costs and benefits. However, we can at least say that the turn of the millennium represented a time when the openness of national economies to international markets (including labour markets) was something that was spoken of by politicians.

The context which gave rise to Operation Vaken and related initiatives was one in which this type of empirical discourse is no longer deemed acceptable, at least where the movement of human beings is concerned. The then Chancellor of the Exchequer, George Osborne, was able to say in early 2016 that the UK economy was vulnerable to a 'cocktail of threats' posed by global economic uncertainties, as if this might strengthen him politically. However, the nature of migration policy and the political position of the Home Office means that the Home Secretary cannot discuss the movement of people in economic or statistical terms, let alone refer to it as something beyond state control. Least of all does it appear as something that can be celebrated. This represents a grave problem for democracy and the public sphere, as migration levels tend to rise and fall in tandem with macroeconomic growth, and the inability to discuss this from what Foucault called the 'perspective of liberal government' means that political rhetoric and policy ends up focused instead on seeking to shape attitudes and emotions of (sections of) the public. Attempts to speak scientifically or realistically about this policy issue are no longer viewed as legitimate by large swathes of the British political class.

Postliberalism does not offer a new paradigm of governmentality, as its purpose is to attack the very idea of centralised, technocratic, statistically informed government. It does however suggest that policy-makers should become more attuned to the affective, emotional and symbolic dimensions of the state, and become more expert in manipulating how these are seen and felt. Arguably, Operation Vaken was a case of such postliberalism, in which the violent qualities of the sovereign state were displayed in billboard form, in order to impress an alternative sense of toughness, reassurance and fear across particular communities. This postliberalism has certain formal qualities in common with *pre*liberalism, or violent public demonstrations of power as described by Foucault at the opening of *Discipline and Punish* (1991), to the extent that it involves heightened attention to ritual, symbolism and the aesthetics of political action. And yet it also bears the hallmarks of postliberal 'nudging' and 'dog-whistling', in which a message is carefully crafted to communicate in an unconscious or coded fashion with particular groups. Marketing and sovereignty therefore reach new alliances, squeezing out the space of liberalism: the marketing campaign aimed at representing Britain as a 'hostile environment' or the rebranding of the UK borders to look 'tougher' would be examples of such new alliances between the traditional goals of sovereignty and the latest techniques of affective management.

Leaving aside ethical questions, what is epistemologically and technically problematic about this postliberal or neo-communitarian emphasis upon emotional attachments and prejudices is that it is constantly at risk of being found out, given the underlying governmental, statistical and economic reality from which it seeks to distract. The wishful thinking of postliberalism is that nostalgically imagined nationhood, cultural homogeneity and locality can be restored, despite neoliberal trends pulling in the opposite direction. It represents a failure of political discourse to adequately represent the sociological, historical, political and economic forces that produce high levels of migration in the first place, and opts for soothing communitarianism instead. Postliberal rhetoric tends to conceal neoliberal reality but not thwart it. What concerns us is that, in doing so, it further isolates and attacks those citizens and non-citizens who are seen as lacking value in both neoliberal and postliberal terms.

References

Baritz, L. (1960) *The Servants of Power*, Middletown, CT: Wesleyan University Press.

Becker, G.S. (1976) *The Economic Approach to Human Behavior*, Chicago: University of Chicago Press.

Blair, T. (2000) *Speech at the World Economic Forum at Davos, Switzerland*, 18 January, http://webarchive.nationalarchives.gov.uk/20060715135117/number10.gov.uk/page1508 [last accessed 22 May 2016].

Blond, P. (2010) *Red Tory: How Left and Right Have Broken Britain and How We Can Fix It* (Main edition), London: Faber & Faber.

Brown, W. (2015) *Undoing the Demos: Neoliberalism's Stealth Revolution*, Cambridge, MA: MIT Press.

Cabinet Office (2001) *Migration: An Economic and Social Analysis*, London: Her Majesty's Stationery Office.

Davies, W. (2012) 'The emerging neocommunitarianism', *The Political Quarterly*, 83 (4): 767–76.

Davies, W. (2014) *The Limits of Neoliberalism: Authority, Sovereignty and the Logic of Competition*, London: Sage.

Desrosières, A. (1998) *The Politics of Large Numbers: A History of Statistical Reasoning*, Cambridge, MA: Harvard University Press.

Dolan, P., Hallsworth, M., Halpern, D., King, D. and Vlaev, I. (2010) *MINDSPACE: Influencing Behaviour through Public Policy*, London: Institute for Government.

Duffy, B. and Frere-Smith, T. (2014) *Perceptions & Reality: Public Attitudes to Migration*, London: Ipsos MORI.

Farage, N. (2015) 'UKIP's immigration policy is built on fairness', *The Daily Telegraph*, 3 March, www.telegraph.co.uk/news/politics/nigel-farage/11447132/Nigel-Farage-Ukips-immigration-policy-is-built-on-fairness.html [last accessed 22 May 2016].

Faulkner Rogers, J. (2015) 'Are conspiracy theories for (political) losers?', *YouGov*, https://yougov.co.uk/news/2015/02/13/are-conspiracy-theories-political-losers/ [last accessed 15 May 2015].

Foucault, M. (1991) *Discipline and Punish: The Birth of the Prison*, London: Penguin.

Foucault, M. (2007) *Security, Territory, Population: Lectures at the Collège De France, 1977–78*, Basingstoke: Palgrave Macmillan.

Geary, I. and Pabst, A. (2015) *Blue Labour: Forging a New Politics*, London: I.B. Tauris.

Goodhart, D. (2014) *The British Dream: Successes and Failures of Post-War Immigration*, London: Atlantic Books.

Harvey, D. (2005) *A Brief History of Neoliberalism*, Oxford: Oxford University Press.

Home Office (2013) *Operation Vaken Evaluation Report – October 2013*, London: Home Office.

Hutton, A. (2013) 'Exclusive: "sham marriage" police storm real wedding', *Camden New Journal*, 7 November, www.camdennewjournal.com/news/2013/nov/exclusive-sham-marriage-police-storm-real-wedding [last accessed 22 May 2016].

Jones, R., Pykett, J. and Whitehead, M. (2013) *Changing Behaviours: On the Rise of the Psychological State*, Cheltenham: Edward Elgar Publishing.

Katwala, S., Ballinger, S. and Rhodes, M. (2014) *How to Talk about Immigration*, London: British Future.

Painter, C. (2008) 'A government department in meltdown: Crisis at the Home Office', *Public Money and Management*, 28 (5): 275–82.

Rai, S. (2015) 'Political performance: A framework for analysing democratic politics', *Political Studies*, 63 (5): 1179–97.

Riddell, M. (2011) 'Labour's anti-immigration guru', *The Daily Telegraph*, 18 July, www.telegraph.co.uk/news/uknews/immigration/8644334/Labours-anti-immigration-guru.html [last accessed 22 May 2016].

Rose, N. (1996a) *Inventing Our Selves: Psychology, Power, and Personhood*, Cambridge: Cambridge University Press.

Rose, N. (1996b) 'The death of the social? Re-figuring the territory of government', *Economy and Society*, 25 (3): 327–56.

UKIP (2015) 'UKIP launches immigration policy', *UKIP website*, www.ukip.org/ukip_launches_immigration_policy [last accessed 8 July 2016].

Waugh, P. (2016) 'How much do EU migrants cost – or benefit – the UK? "Information not available", minister says', *Huffington Post*, 19 February, www.huffingtonpost.co.uk/2016/02/19/how-much-do-eu-migrants-c_n_9272428.html [last accessed 22 May 2016].

Weaver, M. (2013) 'Bungling immigration officials crash genuine wedding', *The Guardian*, 8 November, www.theguardian.com/uk-news/2013/nov/08/bungling-immigration-sham-wedding-london [last accessed 22 May 2016].

Living Research Three: Migration research and the media

One of the motivations for our project was to use research to intervene in public debates on immigration by providing alternative perspectives on what is often a polarised and entrenched debate where the perspectives of migrants and racially minoritised communities barely feature (Conlan, 2014; Migrant Voice, 2014) and where, as we found, research evidence on 'what works' in managing migration is rarely used by policy-makers. Indeed, the first stage of the project, before it was fully formed or funded, involved an attempt to intervene. As members of a spontaneously formed group of activists, many of the members of the final research team took part in carrying out a street survey which was published in *The Voice* (Chan, 2013), the main Black British newspaper in the UK. Throughout the research project, we communicated our research with the media via press releases, the @MICResearch Twitter feed and our project blog (mappingimmigrationcontroversy.com). The media coverage our project received included *The Telegraph, The Independent, The Financial Times, BBC Woman's Hour, The Herald,* and *Russia Today.* Here, we want to reflect on some of the difficulties of trying to engage with mainstream media when researching contentious issues.

Immigration research in a hostile media environment

The negative tone of debate on immigration in the British media poses particular challenges for communicating research within that context, as it is often a question of how research fits, or does not fit, dominant narratives. Existing research has demonstrated how media coverage of immigration has been marked by moral panics about immigration as a threat to social cohesion and the scapegoating of immigrants for a variety of social anxieties (Hall et al., 1978;

Cohen, 2011; Philo et al., 2013). Immigration has also been associated with criminality through journalists' use of terms such as 'illegal' or 'bogus' (Alia and Bull, 2005) and dehumanisation through the use of terms like 'surge', 'flood' (Joint Committee on Human Rights, 2007, cited in Philo et al., 2013), 'swamp' (*The Sun*, 2002) or 'swarm' (Holehouse, 2015). Government policy as a driver of migration in and from conflict zones, including the UK's role in wars in Iraq or Afghanistan, also tends to be ignored in mainstream media coverage (Lewis et al., 2005 cited in Philo et al., 2013). In *Bad News for Refugees*, Greg Philo and colleagues examined how inflammatory media coverage of asylum seekers and refugees legitimates punitive official public and policy responses, which in turn undermine the sense of identity and security for migrant and racially minoritised communities (Philo et al., 2013). This interaction between inflammatory media coverage and punitive immigration policy can be understood as what Papadopoulos et al. term a 'regime of mobility control', which includes both state and non-state actors, and encompasses processes of observation and action (2008: 163).

This means that trying to translate research into media-friendly formats carries the risk of our research being interpreted within the terms of hegemonic anti-immigrant perspectives, framing what is deemed newsworthy and thus the coverage of research – which, as we found, tends to be selective, focusing narrowly on findings which fit into a polemical rather than data-driven approach, and more specifically an anti-immigration narrative (see examples below). Furthermore, the popularity of UKIP and related populist viewpoints means that those perceived as defending immigration, including academics, become easily dismissed as an out-of-touch liberal metropolitan elite (see Chapter 3) who hold positive views on immigration because they are sheltered from its consequences, in contrast with the beleaguered 'white working class'.[1] This makes it all the more important that we as researchers intervene in debates on immigration. It also means that our research risks being either reduced to pro or con, pigeonholed as coming from an out-of-touch elite, or being misinterpreted.

---

[1] For a challenge to this argument and a discussion of the implications for researchers, see Gunaratnam and Jones (2015) and also Virdee (2014).

Media coverage of our research project

Our project received media coverage from several outlets, but we will focus on a few key examples that illustrate the challenges of communicating research to the media. The first media coverage that our project received was from *The Telegraph*, in response to a press release at the very beginning of the project, and emphasised the fact that we had received £200,000 of *public money* to carry out the research, calling it a 'sizeable grant' (Riley-Smith, 2013), even though this is not a large sum of research funding in relative terms (the budget included paying wages to eight researchers over the 18-month duration of the project, fees to the community organisations, the costs of commissioning the survey, travel costs and other incidentals involved with carrying out the project). The rest of the article focused on the controversy surrounding Operation Vaken and the Go Home van pilot and the fact that the pilot had not been successful. The implication was that our project was problematic because it was using taxpayers' money to criticise government policy – specifically a scheme which had been discontinued – and also because we were seen to be defending immigrants. The organisation Migrants' Rights Network was asked by *The Telegraph* for a negative comment about the project (as it was not one of the project partners) and warned us of the story.

After analysing the results of the Ipsos MORI survey in October 2014 (see Chapter 2 for details) and the first stages of the qualitative research we conducted ourselves, we sent out press releases summarising our interim research findings, which resulted in media coverage in the *Financial Times* and the *Independent* (Jackson, 2014; Green, 2015). Both articles focused on two key findings based on qualitative research:[2] that high-profile government immigration campaigns caused anxiety and unease amongst migrants and those racialised as being from 'Black and minority ethnic' communities, and that they did not even reassure those who were concerned about irregular immigration, leading them to suspect that irregular immigration was worse than they had thought. Other aspects of our findings were left out of the news coverage because they were deemed less newsworthy and/or less conducive to a polemical approach. The *Financial Times* article also cited quotes from the then Home Secretary Theresa May and Immigration Minister James Brokenshire on how the Immigration Bill was

---

[2] Though *The Independent* seemed to confuse this with the Ipsos MORI survey.

making it more difficult for those who did not have a legal right to be in the UK, and how the van pilot was deemed unsuccessful (Jackson, 2014). However, there were no direct responses from the Home Office to our research. The article in the *Independent* emphasised how high-profile immigration campaigns increased racial prejudice. The point was also made that high-profile immigration campaigns made those with legal immigration status and even British citizenship feel unwelcome and reluctant to participate in political activism.

That we were able to put arguments into the mainstream media demonstrating the links between immigration control to racism, and provide evidence about the effects on racially minoritised communities (both are rare), shows the importance of intervening in the media. However, what was more problematic was the *Independent* article's emphasis on 'ethnic minorities' becoming more suspicious of each other:

> Different migrant groups have become increasingly suspicious of one another, with hostility breaking out between asylum seekers, refugees and Eastern Europeans. Some migrants reported ethnic minority British citizens telling them to 'go home'.
>
> (Green, 2015, n.p.)

Passages such as this give the impression of generations of immigrants and settled 'minority ethnic' communities fighting amongst themselves, and it de-emphasises the role of government policy or communications in provoking community tensions, which was also a key finding in our research. It also potentially plays into narratives which claim that anti-immigrant sentiments are not racist because of being expressed by racially minoritised people (for a more detailed discussion of anti-immigrant sentiments amongst racially minoritised communities see Chapter 5).

Human interest stories and the politics of identification

In addition to trying to communicate our research through news media, we also participated in public discussions about the representation of migrants in the media. For example, at a workshop at the Detention Forum Salon in London (in which Hannah and Kirsten participated), Ian Dunt (journalist and editor of the blog *politics.co.uk*) argued that 'politicians, journalists and decision makers still tend to be middle class white men who will identify more with "people like them"' (Jones, 2015). Dunt suggested that advocates for the rights of migrants and asylum seekers should choose human interest stories involving people the British public (or journalists, as gatekeepers to the public) find easy to identify with. This raises questions about how such choices might reproduce hierarchies of class, race, nationality, sexuality, etc. For example, an Australian NHS therapist who suddenly lost her status due to bureaucratic errors was seen to be easier to identify with than a Nigerian asylum seeker who had fled her home country because she faced 14 years in prison for her homosexuality (Jones, 2015). In a blog post about the event, Hannah questioned the terms of identification, and who is seen to be an 'ordinary person'. She asked whether people could imagine themselves or someone they knew being persecuted for their sexuality, and being on the sharp end of the immigration and justice system as a result (see further discussion of this in Chapter 6).

This incident shows the importance for researchers of not only providing alternative viewpoints and evidence but also challenging the terms by which media conventions such as the 'human interest story' operate, and the larger power relations such conventions reflect. As we have discussed, doing so carries the risk of being (mis) interpreted within the terms we wish to challenge. However, within the current political climate, the risk of not intervening in public debates on immigration is more dangerous.

Have you been involved in sharing details of a social research project in the mainstream media? What challenges did you expect? What challenges did you encounter? Did they differ?

In your view, what is the role of academic research in public debate, particularly on controversial issues?

Is media coverage a good way of making academic research findings accessible? Are there different opportunities and risks associated with different forms of media coverage? How might you handle these?

What can be gained by persuading journalists to cover academic research reports? What can be lost?

References

Alia, V. and Bull, S. (2005) *Media and Ethnic Minorities*, Edinburgh: Edinburgh University Press.

Chan, B. (2013) 'Home Office "Go Home" vans were unacceptable', *The Voice*, 23 August, www.voice-online.co.uk/article/home-office-%E2%80%98go-home%E2%80%99-vans-were-%E2%80%98 unacceptable%E2%80%99-says-study [last accessed 22 May 2016].

Cohen, S. (2011) *Folk Devils and Moral Panics: The Creation of the Mods and Rockers*, Abingdon: Taylor and Francis.

Conlan, T. (2014) 'BBC director general launches new diversity plan for corporation', *The Guardian*, 20 June, www.theguardian.com/media/2014/jun/20/bbc-director-general-diversity-plan-minorities-on-air [last accessed 22 May 2016].

Green, C. (2015) 'Immigration policy led to "new forms of racism", says new study', *The Independent*, 1 March, www.independent.co.uk/news/uk/home-news/immigration-policy-led-to-new-forms -of-racism-says-new-study-10078876.html [last accessed 22 May 2016].

Gunaratnam, Y. and Jones, H. (2015) 'Is it fair?', *Mapping Immigration Controversy*, 21 September, http://mappingimmigrationcontroversy.com/2015/09/21/is-it-fair-though-researching-racism-class-and-immigration/ [last accessed 22 May 2016].

Hall, S., Crichter, C., Jefferson, T., Clarke, J. and Roberts, B. (1978) *Policing the Crisis: Mugging, the State and Law and Order*, Basingstoke: Palgrave Macmillan.

Holehouse, M, (2015) 'Calais crisis: Deport more migrants to stop "swarm" crossing Mediterranean, says David Cameron', *The Telegraph*, 30 July, http://www.telegraph.co.uk/news/worldnews/europe/france/11772297/Calais-crisis-Deport-more-migrants-to-stop-swarm-crossing-Mediterranean-says-David-Cameron.html [last accessed 22 May 2016].

Jackson, G. (2014) 'UK measures to tackle illegal immigration increase anxiety', *Financial Times*, 24 November, www.ft.com/cms/s/0/4890fb18-73c8-11e4-92bc-00144feabdc0.html [last accessed 22 May 2016].

Jones, H. (2015) 'Ordinary people', *Mapping Immigration Controversy*, 17 June, http://mappingimmigrationcontroversy.com/2015/06/17/ordinary-people/ [last accessed 22 May 2016].

Migrant Voice (2014) *Migrant Voice UK Media-Monitoring Research: Migrant Voices in Migration Stories*, London: Migrant Voice, www.scribd.com/doc/229372612/Migrants-Invisible-in-UK-Media#scribd [last accessed 22 May 2016].

Papadopoulos, D., Stevenson, N. and Tsianos, V. (2008) *Escape Routes: Control and Subversion in the 21st Century*, London: Pluto Press.

Philo, G., Bryant, E. and Donald, P. (2013) *Bad News for Refugees*, London: Pluto Press.

Riley-Smith, B. (2013) ' "Go Home" van research gets £200,000 grant', *The Telegraph*, 18 November, www.telegraph.co.uk/news/politics/

10457811/Go-Home-vans-research-gets-200000-grant.html   [last accessed 22 May 2016].

The Sun (2002) 'No to asylum "swamp" ', *The Sun*, www.thesun.co.uk/sol/homepage/news/150388/No-to-asylum-swamp.html   [last accessed 22 May 2016].

Virdee, S. (2014) *Racism, Class and the Racialised Outsider*, Basingstoke: Palgrave Macmillan.

4

Spaces and places of governance and resistance

Amaal: I came to live in Barking and Dagenham twenty-five years
ago and at that time ... very few black and Asian and ethnic
minority communities ... and within a short space of I would say
maybe five years or so the borough has changed dramatically and
quite a lot of migrants arrived and that created a little bit more
tension within the wider community and evidently you can see
the changes, you know, people say 'Oh, nothing's changed', but
you can actually see the presence of people, family influx are
coming in, but what we know as an organisation is that these
people arriving in Barking and Dagenham, not necessarily come
from abroad, you know, it is quite a mix. Some of them came [to]
inner city London and moved to Westminster borough and Isling-
ton and those areas, where the cost of living is quite high and the
rent has gone up and people cannot afford in private to rent. So
those are families that are being really pushed from inner cities
to outer London that we know and some really as far as, they
come from within East London, Tower Hamlets and people who
come to Barking and Dagenham from Tower Hamlets now also
and other boroughs in Waltham Forest where there is cheaper
houses here and affordable to live in Barking and Dagenham. But
not everybody sees that, we know, because we have some of these
families accessing our services, but people think, you know, that
these people are new arrivals and they're just sort of off the plane
and just arrived in Barking and Dagenham, but there's quite a
big difference and the majority of them, they are resident in the
UK, but just came to Barking and Dagenham because of the
cheaper and affordable housing.

(Barking and Dagenham Activist Interview,
conducted by Yasmin)

The philosopher and social theorist Michel Foucault once said, 'We
are in an epoch of simultaneity: we are in an epoch of juxtaposition,

the epoch of the near and far, of the side-by-side, of the dispersed' (1986: 22). He might well have been in a conversation with Amaal, a community worker in Barking and Dagenham, quoted above. Amaal's observations of her local area – how it has changed over the years, how there are more complex histories and lives beneath appearances – tells us something important about space and place in modern urban life. As places heave and pulsate with social changes and the proximities of all sorts of differences, we can also cling to place to provide some stable and idealised sense of belonging, community and home (Bammer, 1992; Probyn, 1996).

In this chapter we explore some of these themes and the role of spaces and places in the implementation and reception of, and resistance to, immigration policing campaigns. First, the chapter examines the spaces where the campaigns have intervened, from people's homes, to the street, to cyber space. Building on the argument that such interventions are closely tied to the increasingly domestic nature of border practices as part of a highly visible performance politics (see Chapters 2 and 3), this chapter focuses on the intended and unintended consequences of campaigns. These include acts of resistance, increased fear and feelings of exclusion.

For us the spaces where these anti-immigration interventions (and reactions to them) unfold are not mere backdrops to action. Because space is alive, dynamic and relational, it is always affecting and being affected by what happens in it (Massey, 1994; Lefebvre, 1991). As we argued in Chapter 2, immigration campaigns seek to intervene in political space (Lefebvre, 1991: 33). Here, we look more closely at how campaigns such as Operation Vaken, and resistance to them, feed into the production of particular spaces, for example the intensification of fear associated with the street and with the waiting room at the local Home Office reception centre. It is also the case that the history and meanings of particular places have been mobilised to resist these campaigns.

Drawing on interviews and focus groups carried out in our six UK case study areas (Glasgow, Bradford, East London, West London, Birmingham/Coventry and Cardiff), we highlight how local and national contexts come to matter in how immigration policing campaigns are experienced and interpreted. Here local issues, such as histories of migration and resistance, and national contexts, such as debates about devolution and the 2014 Scottish Independence referendum, impact on reactions to anti-immigration campaigns. Whereas in Ealing and Hounslow (West London), for example, the Go Home van's appearance played into divisive discourses of respectability among established migrants and British citizens (discussed in Chapter

5), in Glasgow opposition to Operation Vaken fed into debates about Scottish Independence.

This chapter argues for the importance of considering the following when examining the impact of anti-immigration campaigns across the UK:

1 the specific characteristics of sites of intervention and resistance
2 how local contexts shape reaction and resistance and, conversely,
3 how anti-immigration campaigns feed into the production of spaces and places.

Place matters: vans in the street, raids on the home

The 'hostile environment' of Operation Vaken and associated initiatives was a multilayered campaign intruding into different kinds of spaces: from the virtual environment to the street, to the intimate spaces of people's homes. These spaces became interlinked as social media were used to circulate information about Vaken's activities in the street and to organise counter-actions (see Living Research Five) – and, as we shall discuss below, the realms of the street and the digital also became interlinked through resistance to these campaigns.

The Go Home vans were possibly the most public aspect of the government's increasingly hard line on immigration, intervening directly in the streets of several ethnically diverse London neighbourhoods (Hounslow, Barking and Dagenham, Ealing, Barnet, Brent and Redbridge). Promising a sense of security that 'something is being done' about an invisible bogeyman (while reinforcing a feeling that the bogeyman lurks among them/us), the impact of the Go Home van travelled beyond the localities through which the vans drove via extensive media coverage. When considering the intervention that the vans made in London, it is not only the wider context of the city as 'global' (Sassen, 1991), or 'superdiverse' (Vertovec, 2007) that matters but how this is lived within the specific contexts of the neighbourhoods where the vans and their message were experienced.

We conducted research in three of the boroughs where the van was piloted: Ealing, Hounslow and Barking and Dagenham. Activists in these areas reported how the vans exacerbated existing tensions in the community. For example, in Barking where feelings on immigration run high, an activist explained:

Amaal: The Go Home vans affected the area, because Barking and Dagenham was one of the areas that was targeted, in terms of the migrant community, I mean, you know, with all the incidents that happened ... 'Go home', that sentence, really that resentment people feel and that is if someone's going to be racist, that is the sentence people are really angry about and feel quite violated if someone says to them 'go home' and for the Government to come up with that ... that is a green light for others to use [it] as well. So that was one of the things that really caused tension in Barking and Dagenham for both communities at that time.

> (Barking and Dagenham Activist Interview,
> conducted by Yasmin)

The specific context of Barking and Dagenham is important here. It is a London borough that has seen a massive loss of jobs, most notably at the Ford factory, which went from employing forty thousand people at its peak in the 1950s to four thousand in 2009 (Hudson, 2009 cited in Simmons, 2014). It has a pressurised housing market, fuelled by the reduction in social rented housing following Thatcher's 1980s institution of the right to buy council properties without the power for local authorities to replace their housing stock (Asthana, 2010). The area has seen significant demographic change in terms of the ethnicity of the residents – the White British population decreased from 81 per cent in 2001 to 49 per cent in 2011 (London Borough of Barking and Dagenham, n.d.). In the early 2000s Barking and Dagenham was targeted by the far right, culminating in the British National Party becoming the official opposition to the Labour council in the elections of 2006, although it lost these seats in 2010. Jones argues that after the 2006 election: 'The borough came to symbolize, for both national press and policy practitioners across the country, the problem of far right mobilisation among the white working class' (2013: 43).

This local context matters when considering the impact of the Go Home van. To return to the interview extract, the van circulating in this locality upset those who are imagined as part of the 'migrant community', by echoing the language of the far right. It exacerbated a division between those who might say 'go home' and those who might be on the receiving end of these comments. The van thus feeds into the formation of and antagonism between what Amaal terms 'the two communities'. As the next chapter will explore in more detail, this division between two imagined communities does not correspond neatly to lines of 'race'. As another activist told us:

Ceebla: We've had political leaders, councillors defect in Barking and Dagenham to UKIP, who are from a minority ethnic background and it's incredible, it is absolutely incredible and on the basis that there are too many Eastern Europeans, it's just, it's so concerning that people are buying into this.

(Barking and Dagenham Activist Interview, conducted by Yasmin)

Interestingly, within this context the van did little to reassure those who held anti-immigration opinions. Participants in a focus group of white British women supporters of the UK Independence Party (UKIP), who describe themselves as being 'in the indigenous minority', dismissed the van as a waste of money:

Annie: It just shows you how stupid this government is.
Chris: It is.
Annie: To think that any illegal person is going to read that and go home ... not in a million years.

(Barking Focus Group, conducted by Yasmin)

So, for these women in this local context, the Go Home van also symbolises an out-of-touch government engaged in local theatrics that is not responding to what they feel is the real issue, for them, 'controlling the borders' (see also Chapters 2 and 3).

Meanwhile, on the other side of London, in Ealing and Hounslow, a focus group discussion with women of South Asian, African and Caribbean origin revealed a slippage between the understanding of the Go Home van's campaign (which four women in the group had seen) and vans that had been seen taking part in immigration raids:

Rita: It's so racist, I can say in my words, it's like we are Asian, we are from other country like Nigeria, Pakistan, India, so why is it only for us? It's coming in my mind straight away, it's showing so much racism.
Sukhwant: Why do you think it's directed at Asian and African communities? Is there something on this that suggests to you?
Rita: Because they grab the people, if you are walking in the street like me and other white people, they grab the Asian first, they don't ask any questions to white people ... they grab the people who have a dark complexion.

(Ealing and Hounslow Focus Group, conducted by Sukhwant)

The van is interpreted as 'racist' by this group because of its associations with immigration enforcement vans that 'grab' people rather than because of the messages displayed on the van. This slippage shows how anti-immigration interventions are not interpreted in a vacuum but rather interact with each other. In this local context, where raids are visible and frequent, vans mean raids.

The issue of raids loomed large in the two focus groups conducted in Ealing and Hounslow. Raids and checks in the street had major impacts on how public spaces were experienced. Even those who had leave to remain in the UK expressed anxiety about being stopped at transport hubs. Rita also described how she panicked when she saw UK Border Agency (UKBA)[1] officers and dogs at the exit barriers of a London railway station (see Chapter 2). She became so nervous that she turned away from the exit barriers and jumped on a train. In this panic, she boarded the wrong train and when she eventually reached home she stayed indoors for some time because of a fear that her leave to remain might be revoked.

In the West London focus groups immigration enforcement was also seen as a threat to even the most intimate of spaces. Women in the Ealing and Hounslow focus groups talked about the frightening experience of having their homes raided. Others had seen them happening nearby, as Iram recounted:

> Iram: I also saw immigration raids in Southall. Where I was living an illegal young man was also living. He was sleeping and they came and took him from his home. These raids are happening quite a lot in Southall and I was scared.
>
> (Ealing and Hounslow Focus Group, conducted by Sukhwant, translation)

It was not only UKBA which was making incursions into the focus group participants' homes. Anjum, also in Ealing and Hounslow, remembered how her child was frightened by the landlord's constant intrusions:

> Anjum: [He] used to knock the room twice a day and used to say we want copies of the passport and we want to know how long your sister is going to stay ... my little son was so much scared that he still doesn't meet that man [and] he has a problem in that house, he doesn't go downstairs when that 'uncle' is there.
>
> (Ealing and Hounslow Focus Group, conducted by Sukhwant)

---

[1] UK Border Agency was the part of the Home Office responsible for border control between 2008 and April 2013, when it was split into UK Visas and Immigration, and Immigration and Enforcement agencies.

These stories from Ealing and Hounslow evoke something of the cumulative effect of the layering up of anti-immigration interventions in multiple places at different scales – the home, the street – and the experience that no place is safe. Several participants wept as they considered the implications of this hostile environment for themselves and for people they know. From witnessing night-time raids in shared houses to seeing people on the street being carted off, they talked about the visceral impact of immigration policy on their lives and their new or increasing sense of precariousness.

The public and policy image of Ealing and Hounslow is rather different to Barking and Dagenham. Whereas Barking and Dagenham has become shorthand for community tensions and far-right success, Ealing incorporates Southall, an area that was used as a good example of community cohesion by the government in the past (Cantle, 2001). More widely, Ealing and Hounslow are home to a number of long-standing civil society organisations for which highlighting and opposing the racist dimension of immigration policy has been a key focus for decades. There is a large South Asian population in both of these boroughs.[2] However, as described in the next chapter, heightened government and media attention to immigration has been divisive, including within the South Asian populations of these boroughs (see also Living Research One). Rita reflected on her experience of negative reactions during a protest against immigration enforcement:

Rita: SBS [Southall Black Sisters] took action against that van and I was with them, we were doing the campaign outside the Himalaya Palace and I was shocked, my Asian community they hate us. They were saying so many people, they are fighting, arguing with me now, and other people, they are saying 'why are you supporting them? They have to go home.' And I was shocked, my community hate me so what can I expect from British people? Of course they are going to be racist with me, they are going to hate me. If my community people they hate me, so who is going to

---

[2] The 2011 Census figures for Ealing put the biggest ethnic group as White English/Welsh/Scottish/Northern Ireland/British (30.4%), with the next biggest single category as White Other (15.4%) followed by Asian/Asian British: Indian (14.3%). For Hounslow, the 2011 Census shows that 37.9% of the population identify as White English/Welsh/Scottish/Northern Ireland/British, with the next largest group who identify as Asian/Asian British: Indian (19%), followed by 11.5% who identify as White Other. Source: Office for National Statistics, Neighbourhood Statistics table 'Ethnic Group (KS201EW): London'.

accept us? So of course it's impacting my community, they have split us. My Asian community hate Asian people, it was so sad.

(Ealing and Hounslow Focus Group,
conducted by Sukhwant)

In this case the lines drawn are not between resident and migrant but between 'good (established) migrant' and 'bad (new) migrant' (how this becomes discussed through the language of who is 'deserving' and 'undeserving' will be further explored in Chapter 5). In both East and West London the vans fuelled anti-migrant sentiments and divisions but, because of different histories of migration, this was interpreted and experienced differently. The imagined figure of the migrant 'other' is different in the two contexts. This depends on who the newcomers are in each community – the figure of the 'unrespectable' South Asian in West London, and the Eastern European in Barking and Dagenham, for instance.

But this government messaging did not circulate only on the streets of London. While the Go Home van element of Operation Vaken was implemented only in London, 26 per cent of Ipsos MORI's survey sample (see Appendix) was aware of it, making it the most visible aspect of the communications campaigns we asked about nationally. The Go Home van was covered extensively in the UK press, thus circulating far beyond the neighbourhoods through which it was driven. This led to some confusion among our respondents about the exact places of intervention (see below).

In addition, the official Home Office Twitter account began to share photographs of immigration officers apprehending people, leading them in handcuffs into the back of enforcement vans, with text such as #immigrationoffender and #nohidingplace. After substantial criticism (see Living Research Five), the Home Office quickly moved to a softer, less aggressive Twitter voice, focusing on missing persons and violence against women. But this short-lived social media strategy enabled the virtual circulation of these highly visible localised raids and therefore their use as anti-immigration propaganda. The tactic of making raids visible also included locally targeted actions such as taking journalists from local papers along to immigration raids on weddings, workplaces and homes (see Chapter 3).

At the same time, a more private poster campaign was taking place. The Brand Street (Glasgow) and Hounslow (London) Immigration Enforcement reporting offices were saturated with posters and stickers on the walls, chairs and floor, asking 'Is life here hard? Going home is simple,' accompanied by images of destitute people. There were also mobiles of planes hung from the ceiling. This campaign was much less public than the street-level interventions in London and was targeted at those already in a vulnerable position within the immigration system.

The adverse effects of displaying these posters in a place that is already feared by those who use it were described in focus groups in Ealing and Hounslow. When asked by Sukhwant about who in the group had seen the van, Angela's response was directly related to the reporting office poster campaign:

> Angela: Yes not only on the bus, it was also in Home Office because I used to go in there, to sign on.
> Sukhwant: The reception centres?
> Angela: Yeah … So when I went there, and saw it, oh – I just can't describe how I felt because I thought they put it here because they want to scare every single person. And it wasn't very good.
> (Ealing and Hounslow Focus Group, conducted by Sukhwant)

As we also heard in Chapter 3, the posters in the reception centre add to fear within an already intimidating situation.

In Glasgow, where the Home Office posters were displayed without the van campaign, some of the focus group of asylum seekers and refugees had seen them in person but another person in the group refused to believe that this had happened in Glasgow – 'that was in London, not here' said one of the participants. In exploring why 'not here', the national context of Scotland becomes important.

National matters: telling Immigration Enforcement to 'Go Home'

We now zoom out from these smaller places and localities to consider how anti-immigration campaigns intervened in national contexts in the different countries of the UK, focusing particularly on Scotland and Wales where anti-immigration campaigns were used to draw distinctions between the countries in the UK.

The timing in Scotland was particularly significant, as the campaign unfolded in the run up to the 2014 Scottish Independence referendum. The Home Office reporting centre posters in Glasgow in particular and the campaign in general became reference points in the referendum campaign. The reaction to the campaign in Scotland was very negative. Key to the counter-campaign in Scotland was the argument that the posters were an intolerant Westminster imposition on (a more welcoming) Scotland. The *Herald* newspaper published an editorial that argued: 'The Scottish Parliament should make clear that this kind of behaviour is not acceptable in Scotland. Perhaps it's time to tell the UKBA to "Go home" ' (Herald View, 2013). This is just one example of how the campaign was used to distinguish between a punitive British state and a possible alternative Scottish approach, one that combines pro-immigration policies and civic nationalism. This also perhaps accounts for why one focus group participant from Glasgow refused to believe that the posters were displayed in Scotland ('that was London, not here').

The Scottish National Party (SNP) argued that UK policy on asylum and immigration was not in keeping with Scottish attitudes or the proposals for immigration and asylum in *Scotland's Future* (the White Paper on independence) that also included the proposal to close Dungavel Immigration Detention Centre. The White Paper explicitly references the 'Go Home' campaign to highlight these disparities:

> It is [also] difficult to conceive of a Scottish government that would ever adopt the crude 'go home' approach tried by the current Westminster Government.
>
> (The Scottish Government, 2013: 255–6)

Thus an inhospitable UK is held up against a welcoming Scotland and a promise of a fairer society to come. This position was echoed in a debate held in the Scottish Parliament in December 2013 on the poster campaign. All speakers of all political parties condemned the campaign but all SNP speakers used opposition to the campaign to stress the need for Scottish independence.

In a focus group carried out with refugees and asylum seekers in Glasgow we found strident pro-independence views. However, this seemed not to rely on feelings of belonging to Scotland as such, but rather on the specific policies on migration and asylum set out in the White Paper and on the idea of the Scottish state as generally more sympathetic than the Westminster government:

> Sirvan: There is not any guarantee for new Scotland, or independent Scotland, that make life easy for refugees or asylum seekers, but still we believe that would be better because there is a campaign to support asylum or refugees. So the number of the population of Scotland is quite small, so it's quite easy to fight with the Parliament, you know Edinburgh Parliament, Scottish Parliament instead of UK.
>
> Theresa: Because all the rules you are using here in Scotland ... the Home Office, their rules, they are from England.
>
> (Glasgow focus group, conducted by Emma)

In this focus group discussion, once again the Home Office is associated with the UK state (and equated with English dominance) rather than the Scottish government, which is characterised here as easier to access. Within this narrative of a more welcoming Scotland, we also found Glasgow to have a particular resonance (explored further below).

Although this was less pronounced in Wales, there was discussion in the focus groups about how immigration enforcement campaigns were largely Home Office, and therefore English, initiatives. In one of the activist interviews, Alex reflected on the situation of refugees and asylum seekers in Wales:

> Alex: Compared to the rest of the UK, the situation in Wales is not as good as it is in Scotland, but it's better than the situation in England.
>
> (Cardiff Activist Interview, conducted by Roiyah)

Debates on immigration in Wales have not had the same vehemence as in England, perhaps because of different and earlier patterns of immigration centred on the port city of Cardiff and dating back to the late nineteenth century (see Harries, 2015).

However, unlike Glasgow, in Cardiff devolution was not extensively discussed. The mood among immigration activists towards devolution was less positive than in the Glasgow research, and more sceptical opinions were voiced. One activist commented:

> Crystal: Wales Government has no power [over immigration] but where they have the powers what did they do? Education, health, housing, community cohesion, what do they do? What has come out of it? What has come out of it? I don't know. I'm asking, what has come out of it?
>
> (Cardiff Activist Interview, conducted by Roiyah)

There were significant differences between how the campaign fed in, or not, to debates about devolution in these two countries. In Scotland, the presence of the posters within Scotland itself, and in the local context of Glasgow as the country's most ethnically diverse city, during a time of fervent debate about Scotland's place in the United Kingdom made the posters highly symbolic of an unsympathetic state intruding on Scottish soil. Although Cardiff is also unusually ethnically diverse within Wales, here the campaign was not physically present but experienced via social media and the news. Unlike in Scotland, debate on devolution was not particularly heightened and so the campaign did not feed into discussions of nationhood in the same way.

History matters: reaction and resistance

Within these national debates, other more local forms of belonging are drawn upon in terms of resistance and mobilisation against anti-immigration campaigns. This was particularly noticeable in Cardiff and Glasgow, multicultural hubs in countries that are otherwise more ethnically homogenous than is England. In the Cardiff interviews and focus groups, the overwhelming majority of participants perceived Cardiff as different from other places in being more welcoming, friendlier and safer. The general street level conviviality, and the urban 'multicultured' areas, places and streets in which to socialise, worship and 'hang out' were noted as contributing factors. In this extract from a Cardiff focus group, Omar argues that anti-immigration campaigns do not have much impact on Cardiff:

> Omar: I personally would think that Cardiff was a community itself. That would more or less bring them, bring the community together closer. And speaking from my experience because of the diversity and the way it's changed going ten years back. You work with Polish people, Turkish people, Moroccans and you work with the guy from the valleys, pure Welsh boy and you got someone from Ireland, you know Scottish, and they're all there. So who's going to say he's not from here? Who's going to say who should go, the Scottish guy, or the Moroccan, or should we all pick on the Irish guy or me, the black man?
>
> (Cardiff focus group, conducted by Roiyah)

Omar's feeling is that because of the diversity in Cardiff, picking off specific groups as 'others', not entitled to belong, would not work. As well as this long-standing history of migration and multiculture, the twin factors of an increase in numbers of those seeking asylum in Cardiff since 2001 (since the policy of dispersal was introduced which moved thousands of asylum seekers to cities around the UK, in an attempt to ease pressure on services in London and south-east England) and the erosion of asylum seekers' rights have given rise to a wave of refugee-related activism in the city (Payson, 2015). The well-established anti-racist presence in Cardiff was another contributing factor. In the following exchange with Roiyah, Crystal, an activist in Cardiff, considers whether the van campaign would have been possible there:

> Crystal: No, they couldn't even bring in to Cardiff anyway.
> Roiyah: What, do you think it wouldn't have worked if they had the vans going up and down?
> Crystal: It won't work. We are so barbaric in Wales it cannot work.
> (Cardiff Activist Interview 2, conducted by Roiyah)

Here 'barbaric' refers to the stridency of local activism.

Like Cardiff, Glasgow has responded to the dispersal of asylum seekers in the city through pro-migrant activism. In Glasgow, work by local statutory organisations and community campaigns to address tensions and anti-migrant feeling and incidents was galvanised by the murder of an asylum seeker, Firsat Dag, in the city in 2001. Community-led campaigns to protect asylum seekers, such as the 'Glasgow Girls'[3] campaigns, arose following this, particularly as people became integrated into local communities, importantly through attending school together. These networks have many characteristics of long-standing trade union and political organising that have strong traditions in the city. The campaigns have been important in galvanising politicians' and others' characterisations of Glasgow as being hospitable to newcomers.

Ideas of Glasgow (rather than just Scotland) as a particularly welcoming place in contrast to a hostile Home Office were also drawn on to counter the 'Go Home' campaign, in political speeches at demonstrations ('Glasgow is a welcoming city. It will take anyone to its heart that will love Glasgow back ... The only people we don't welcome is UKBA', Nina Baker, Green Party councillor, Emma's fieldnotes, 9 September 2013) and in an editorial in *The Herald* newspaper:

> This attempt to intimidate asylum seekers in Glasgow seems to be of the same Home Office mindset. This is particularly offensive

---

[3] The 'Glasgow Girls' are a group of seven young women who first got together to campaign against the detention of one of their school friends, an asylum seeker whose claim had been refused. This grew into a campaign for the rights of all children asylum seekers. Their story was made into a musical which was then turned into a musical drama for the BBC (see Scottish Refugee Council, n.d.).

because Glasgow has a proud history of welcoming refugees into the local community without the kind of friction that has been seen in some parts of the country.

(Herald View, 2013)

Such feelings were not only expressed by politicians and the media. There was a general feeling among the focus group with asylum seekers and refugees in Glasgow that Glasgow was a friendly place, that people there were accepting and that, although there was racism, it was better than other places. People talked about living in areas that were stigmatised and said that, although others thought these were bad places, for them this was home. Roselin, an asylum seeker from Zimbabwe, said:

> People say Ibrox[4] is a dangerous place to be, but to me I have never experienced that. I have been in that same place. For more than three years I have stayed in Glasgow, so it is like my birth home.
>
> (Glasgow Focus Group, conducted by Emma)

In research in Glasgow for a previous project (AMICALL based at COMPAS, University of Oxford), Hannah was told by an officer in the local authority that the UK Border Agency had informed him that they found Glasgow to be the most difficult city in the UK from which to deport people whose asylum claims had been rejected. This was due to community-organised resistance campaigns which had physically prevented officers from entering properties to remove people, as well as mounting public demonstrations and letter-writing campaigns (Jones, 2012). This opposition between Glasgow activists and the Home Office is echoed in our current research by an activist who suggested that the decision to pilot the 'Go Home' posters in Glasgow might have been the Home Office testing whether pro-refugee activists were still able to mobilise:

> Jean: I think from time to time they just, they're putting out feelers, 'have they finally got tired of it, has it finally calmed down up there?'
>
> (Glasgow Activist Interview, conducted by Emma)

There are similarities in this excerpt with the Cardiff discussion of people being too 'barbaric' to accept a campaign like the vans. As

---

[4]A neighbourhood in Glasgow.

such, Glasgow and Cardiff are presented as rebellious places, kicking against the government.

The particular histories of Glasgow and Cardiff as places of resistance – and as centres of dispersed asylum seekers – are important. Among the English case studies, we have found similar comparisons between cities with a good support infrastructure for refugees and those without. For example, in a Bradford focus group, Lucee explained:

> I used to live in Leeds when I first came because I lived mainly in London and then I was brought to Leeds by the Immigration, and I found like in Leeds there was a few supporting groups, there weren't as many, they weren't like outreaching; when I came to Bradford I just found it's totally different, multicultural; I can get food from my country, you know like, there's all sorts going on, you know. And then there's all these support groups, you know, there was the BAFR, I mean Bradford Action for Refugees, Red Cross, BIASAN, together, I mean there are so many projects, so I found, yeah, in Bradford there is more support and obviously being in the City, centrally it's good.
>
> (Bradford Focus Group, conducted by Hannah)

Like Glasgow and Cardiff, Bradford is a resettlement area for people seeking asylum. In the national imagination, Bradford tends to be discussed as a touchstone of community unrest associated with tensions between British Muslims and white British communities, centring on moments such as the burning of Salman Rushdie's *The Satanic Verses* and controversy about the racist headmaster Ray Honeyford in the 1980s (Burnett, 2009); riots in the 1980s and 2001 (Hussain and Bagguley, 2005; Pearce and Bujra, 2011) and recent mobilisations of the far-right and anti-Muslim English Defence League (EDL) (Treadwell, 2012). For activists we spoke to in the area, the major areas of unrest or worry tended to be around far-right mobilisations, with incidents in 2013 including UKIP electoral mobilisation and EDL provocations at mosques, rather than the Home Office migration rhetoric. However, the comments of refugees, asylum seekers and others also pointed to ways that immigration enforcement intervened in their daily lives, even if it was less visible in everyday public discourse of others. Similarly, Lucee's view, quoted above, of finding Bradford a relatively well-organised place in terms of refugee and asylum seeker support, contrasted with some activist views about local political organising. Pete, an activist Hannah interviewed in Bradford who had been involved in labour and migration politics in the area for decades, described the city as having plenty of people who would come to nostalgic film screenings about the miners' strike, but a more difficult place to mobilise demonstrations or direct action towards austerity or other current concerns.

Similarly, in the West Midlands an issue that emerged in interviews with activists was the difference between Birmingham and Coventry in terms of migrant and refugee organising. Coventry seemed to be a more conducive environment than Birmingham, which some saw as connected to Coventry's history as a city of peace and reconciliation. By contrast, organising in Birmingham seemed to be particularly difficult due to the fragmented layout of the city, as well as pressures for voluntary sector organisations (not limited to Birmingham) to adopt a 'servicing model' – whereby immigration professionals act on behalf of migrants and asylum seekers rather than migrants and asylum seekers advocating on their own behalf. Accounts emerged in one of the interviews about how Home Office imperatives to create a 'hostile environment' (see Chapter 2) were making it more difficult for voluntary sector organisations to support migrants and asylum seekers.[5] In these English cities (Bradford, Coventry and Birmingham) the 'Go Home' messaging was experienced – and responded to – as less of a spectacular event and more as an adding of another layer to an already difficult situation for asylum seekers and refugees.

In contrast, perhaps the most immediate and spectacular moment of resistance we saw during the research was the Southall Black Sisters' spontaneous protest at Himalaya Palace, and its video recording (Malhi TV, 2013). As in Glasgow, this event provides an example of how long-standing anti-racist organisations can challenge divisive politics and mobilise networks of solidarity relatively quickly.

Some of the women who later contributed to the Ealing and Hounslow focus group discussions had been meeting at Southall Black Sisters (SBS), a women's centre in West London, and discussing media coverage of migration, cuts in access to welfare, proposals that welfare benefits claimants should undergo English language tests, government statements about restricting student entry into the country and proposals for the 2014 Immigration Bill (since passed

---

[5] Indeed, during our research two of the groups we were working with, Birmingham Asylum and Refugee Association (BARA) and Coventry Asylum and Refugee Action Group (CARAG), both lost their core funding after the Regional Asylum Association decided they would no longer fund self-organised asylum seekers' groups. However, BARA subsequently received £8,000 from the Lottery Fund.

into law). The women viewed these developments as deeply worrying and inhumane and they discussed ways in which they could protest against these incursions. This was when an immigration enforcement van pulled up a few doors from the SBS centre's offices, and simmering unease ignited into spontaneous action.

A quick consensus was reached to go out on to the street to protest. The women scribbled slogans on to pieces of A3 paper, grabbed a megaphone, and started shouting 'UKBA go away'. They also decided it was important to warn local residents of the likelihood of a raid by sounding the alarm 'if you are illegal, run, leave the area, there's a raid going on!' (in Hindi). The women then followed the van to a small shopping centre. Enforcement officers had sealed the entrance to the shopping centre and they were questioning the small businesses and predominantly South Asian workers inside.

In a quick subversion of the Home Office agenda, they enacted their own 'hostile environment' by demonstrating at the entrance to the building and using a megaphone to amplify their opposition – these officers were being made unwelcome and ashamed of what they were doing. They also made a point of shouting in Hindi so that local people could understand what was going on. Dozens of local shoppers and passers-by encircled the demonstrators, in solidarity or simply out of curiosity. Some of them voiced contrary opinions and some heated discussions ensued.

In this moment the street was seized, reclaimed and reorganised or 'reconstituted' as an offensive against anti-immigration controls. Furthermore, the YouTube video of this protest went viral. An image of one of the SBS workers became the logo for a network of activists – the Anti Raids Network – issuing similar calls to join them in protest against immigration raids across London.

Whose streets, whose place?

Our research has shown how anti-immigration campaigns can make people more fearful about immigration. Here we have explored how place matters within these processes. We began by looking at the specific places where the Go Home van circulated. In these London boroughs the van was not experienced in a vacuum, but rather was experienced and interpreted within other neighbourhood struggles and histories and, in conjunction with other anti-immigration interventions. So in Barking and Dagenham this fed into feelings of 'us and them' (Anderson, 2013) – a division between migrants and non-migrants. In Ealing and Hounslow, the van exacerbated frictions within the South Asian population, while protests against it gave voice to an alternative perspective (see also Chapter 5).

Perhaps unsurprisingly, the places where the vans circulated and/ or posters had been displayed are the places where we found most street-level opposition to the campaigns. Just as Twitter was used as a space for Home Office enforcement and was then reclaimed as a space for parody and organising (including the beginnings of this research project – see Living Research Five), in both Glasgow and Ealing and Hounslow protests sought to reclaim these localities through visible street protests. In Glasgow, this took the form of gathering behind the campaign banner 'Glasgow Campaign to Welcome Refugees' and cheering on speakers who promoted the idea of Glasgow as a welcoming place. In protests in Ealing and Hounslow, Southall Black Sisters proclaimed 'Whose streets? Our streets'. It should be emphasised that in both places these protests were not one-off events but came from networks with long-standing histories of protest and organising on immigration and refugee issues. Through these examples we can see how anti-immigration campaigns are not just rolled out over a flat terrain but reverberate through particular places differently.

We also saw how Operation Vaken fed into ideas of nation. Primarily and most notably we have explored here how an anti-anti-immigration position was taken by the Scottish National Party (SNP) in the run up to the Scottish Independence Referendum. In this context the posters took on added meaning as symbols of an unwelcoming and remote Westminster-based Home Office, highlighting the difference between a potential independent Scotland and the existing approach to immigration and asylum of the Westminster government. This did not unfold in the same way in Wales. Responses there had more in common with our Bradford and Birmingham case studies where the Operation Vaken campaign was seen as fanning the flames of racism and xenophobia but was not experienced as intensely as the places where the campaigns unfolded.

If we think of spaces as being continually produced, as suggested in the introduction to this chapter, we can also reflect on how immigration enforcement campaigns are a part of the production of space. They contribute to how space is practised (Lefebvre, 1991) – the experience of seeing an anti-immigration van on your local high street and deciding to take a different route tomorrow. They feed into how officials conceive of and represent spaces; think of the van circulating in Barking and Dagenham, stirring up ill feeling and adding to the perception of those watching from afar of a divided community. But crucially they also produce new spaces and platforms for forms of protest and the creation of other ideas of what specific locations could mean, resonating in the chant: 'Whose streets? Our streets!'

References

Anderson, B. (2013) *Us and Them?: The Dangerous Politics of Immigration Control*, Oxford, Oxford University Press.

Asthana, A. (2010) 'Target BNP: A battle for the soul of east London', *The Guardian*, 21 March, www.theguardian.com/politics/2010/mar/21/bnp-dagenham-barking-elections [last accessed 22 May 2016].

Bammer, A. (1992) 'Editorial: The question of "home" ', *New Formations*, 17: vii–xi.

Burnett, J. (2009) 'Racism and the state: authoritarianism and coercion', in R. Coleman, J. Sim, S. Tombs and D. Whyte (eds), *State, Power, Crime*, Los Angeles: Sage, pp. 49–61.

Cantle, T. (2001) *Community Cohesion: A Report of the Independent Review Team*, London: Home Office.

Foucault, M. (1986) 'Of other spaces', *Diacritics*, 16 (1): 22–7.

Harries, B. (2015) ' "Yma o hyd? Gwyn o hyd? (Still here? Still white?)" Racism, identity and nationalism in post-devolution Wales', Paper presented at *Racism and Nationalism after the Scottish Referendum and 2015 General Election*, Birkbeck, London, 11 November.

Herald View (2013) 'Campaign that is not wanted here', *Herald Scotland*, 30 August, www.heraldscotland.com/opinion/13120517.Campaign_that_is_not_wanted_here/ [last accessed 22 May 2016].

Hudson, P. (2009) '80 years of Ford at Dagenham', *The Telegraph*, 15 May, www.telegraph.co.uk/motoring/classiccars/5318900/80-years-of-Ford-at-Dagenham.html [last accessed 22 May 2016].

Hussain, Y. and Bagguley, P. (2005) 'Citizenship, ethnicity and identity: British Pakistanis after the 2001 "riots" ', *Sociology*, 39 (3): 407–25.

Jones, H. (2012) *Attitudes to Migrants, Communication and Local Leadership: Country Research Report – UK*, Oxford: COMPAS.

Jones, H. (2013) *Negotiating Cohesion, Inequality and Change: Uncomfortable Positions in Local Government*, Bristol: Policy Press.

Lefebvre, H. (1991) *The Production of Space*, Oxford: Blackwell.

London Borough of Barking and Dagenham (n.d.) 'Summary of the 2011 Census results for Barking and Dagenham', www.lbbd.gov.uk/council/statistics-and-data/census-information/2011-census/ [last accessed 22 May 2016].

Malhi TV (2013) *Southall Black Sisters Against Enforcement Team in Southall*, YouTube, www.youtube.com/watch?v=pQ0_TFBVots [last accessed 22 May 2016].

Massey, D. (1994) *Space, Place, Gender*, Cambridge: Polity.

Payson, A. (2015) 'Moving feelings, intimate moods and migrant protest in Cardiff', *JOMEC Journal: Journalism, Media and Cultural Studies*, 7: 1–16, http://www.cardiff.ac.uk/jomec/research/journalsandpublications/jomecjournal/7%20-%20june2015/index.html [last accessed 2 February 2016].

Pearce, J. and Bujra, J. (2011) *Saturday Night and Sunday Morning: The Story of the Bradford Riots*, Bradford: Vertical Editions.

Probyn, E. (1996) *Outside Belongings*, London and New York: Routledge.

Sassen, S. (1991) *The Global City: New York, London, Tokyo*, Princeton, Princeton University Press.

Scottish Government (2013) *Scotland's Future: Your Guide to an Independent Scotland*, Edinburgh: The Scottish Government, www.gov.scot/Resource/0043/00439021.pdf [last accessed 22 May 2016].

Scottish Refugee Council (n.d.) 'The Glasgow Girls', www.scottishrefugeecouncil.org.uk/news_and_events/get_involved_in_arts_events/glasgow_girls [last accessed 22 May 2016].

Simmons, D. (2014) *A Study of the Transition to Parenthood in Barking and Dagenham, Examining the Experiences of UK Born and Migrating Parents*, PhD thesis, University of Greenwich.

Treadwell, J. (2012) 'White Riot: The English Defence League and the 2011 English riots', *Criminal Justice Matters*, 87(1): 36–7.

Vertovec, S. (2007) 'Super-diversity and its implications', *Ethnic and Racial Studies*, 30 (6):1024–54.

Living Research Four: Ethics in uncomfortable research situations

The ethical bottom line for sociologists is, 'first, do no harm'. This can mean taking care that how we present our research does not add to raced, classed and gendered oppressions, and equally, avoiding a well-meaning shrug and a response of 'It's complicated'. At its best, sociology takes seriously the personal, everyday struggles and inconsistencies of individuals; but it does this while also keeping in mind the larger structural forces that shape those everyday struggles and give them meaning.

Social life is nuanced and complicated, and capturing and representing this complexity in research is difficult. When producing our analysis we at least have time and space for reflection, for multiple attempts to get it right (or to fail again, but fail better – following Samuel Beckett but also Michael Keith's (2005: 133) application of this formulation to social research). But we can face more immediate challenges in our data generation, which go beyond the questions of informed consent, anonymity, confidentiality and fidelity to the data which are covered by most discussions of research ethics. Often in empirical research we can face unanticipated challenges of how to comport ourselves as researchers, and simply as human beings.

One example of such challenges in our project is illustrated by this extract from Emma's fieldnotes of a focus group she held in Glasgow with asylum seekers and refugees:

Things got very emotional when the older woman from Zimbabwe started talking about her situation, including not being able to afford to repair her broken glasses that are held together with Sellotape, being refused a bus pass and most of all her separation from her children. She is in tears, as are two other members of the group and I am also blinking back tears trying to remain 'the researcher'. I reach for the older woman's hand and hold it for a few minutes while she carries on talking. Her upset is laced with anger at the injustice of her situation. A few minutes later she describes the impossibility of her living situation and then looking me in the eye asks '*would you look after me in your house as well as you would look after yourself?*' I am rather floored by this, even though it is a rhetorical question. But the message is, sympathy is not enough here.

(Emma's fieldnotes)

How would you behave in this situation? If you have been trained as a sociological researcher, you have probably thought about questions such as objectivity, positionality, reflexivity and rapport. But all of this training and reflection in advance cannot remove the discomfort and confusion from moments like this. Moments like this provoke questions about the practices we use to produce data, as well as the meanings of the data. They also, often, force us to think about what it means to be a researcher in these interpersonal situations. How you might behave in this situation depends on who you are, what you have experienced, and your personal and political beliefs, as well as your training as a researcher.

As anti-racist feminist researchers, we have not aimed for objectivity because it seems to us that this is always an illusion. *Objectivity* is the idea that there is a single truth about the way the world exists, which researchers can aim to find, without being biased by their own opinions, experiences or expectations. The idea that any interpretation of the world can be objective has been challenged by theorists who demonstrate that all knowledge is situated – that is, everything we know is informed by our ways of knowing, from the language we use to make sense of the world to the parts of the world we think are important or irrelevant (see e.g. Haraway, 1991; Rose, 1997). Instead, we have sought to recognise our *positionality* – that is, to consider our own role in the research environment and generation of data, alongside the people we are studying. This means recognising that how researchers interpret the world is informed by our training as academic researchers in a particular discipline, who have read and been convinced by certain theories. It also means recognising that our influence on other people and the way we understand and interact with the world is informed by things other than our professional selves – for example, our gender, ethnicity, age, class, accent, the way we dress, the ways we talk to other people, the political and ethical views we hold, our personal values, and our previous experiences. We believe this is true of all research, and so these elements need to be taken into account when we conduct research, and when we analyse what our research encounters mean. This is what is meant by *reflexivity* – not just acknowledging that everyone is positioned differently in relation to knowledge and power (much less, suggesting that as a result any interpretation is equally valid), but recognising that all knowledge is the product of specific relations in specific times and places, and that specificity is part of the essence of understanding and making sense of research.

So what are the specifics of the interaction described in Emma's fieldnotes above, and how can we think about dealing with these kinds of moments as researchers? This was a situation in which a white British researcher employed by a university was in a room with a number of people of varying ethnicities and nationalities, all of whom had come to the UK to seek asylum; some of them had secured refugee status, others were still waiting to see if they would be allowed to stay and therefore very precarious in terms of their legal status, their living conditions and what they could expect in their future. Emma had not met the group before, though a worker from the community group with whom we were conducting the research was there too, and knew others in the group. Emma had explained the reasons for the research to everyone there, explained how we would use the data, asked for their permission to record the meeting and made it clear that they could withdraw if they wished. This is known in researcher jargon as gaining *informed consent* and is partly a way of addressing power inequalities between researchers and those they research, by aiming to ensure that people being researched are willing and know what they are getting into.

Nevertheless, as a result of taking part in the research, the participant became visibly distressed, and explained a painful situation in which she still found herself. The researcher recorded this for use in her work (the story became data), while the participant herself would continue to have to live in this situation. The researcher was sympathetic and tried to express her sympathy (for example, by holding the participant's hand), but then was 'floored' by the recognition of a direct challenge to the value of this sympathy when faced with the material conditions of their different situations.

The reason for pointing to this uneasiness in the research encounter is not to identify ways of (the researcher) being more comfortable with similar situations in future. Nor is the intention to put the researcher (or her feelings) at the centre of the situation, since the purpose of the event was to explore the experiences of the participants. Elsewhere in this book we have tried to show how we have listened to and analysed the experiences and data we gathered for our research, and situated these within wider social structures and power relations. But here we think it might be helpful for other researchers who recognise these 'uneasy' situations we enter and provoke in our work, to think about what it means to practise research in this way – and to think about ways of acting in these very immediate situations when they occur.

There are a few more things to keep in mind when thinking about these uneasy research situations, and the ethics of bringing them about (however inadvertently), acting in the moment, and writing about them afterwards (see also Dreher, 2009). First, the role of the social researcher is important. If Emma had been present at the focus group as someone who could help to fix the research participant's housing or immigration situation, she might have been of more practical help – but she would not have been able to document the longer-term experiences of the group in the way she has as a researcher. One of the values of sociological research is to document social relations, to provide analysis of individual stories and wider trends, and to make the links between these. There is a value in this just as there is a value in the very different role of providing advocacy or support, and as long as it is made clear to participants *why* the researcher is doing what they do, this does not make the encounter 'unethical'.

The notion of informed consent in research is important. Too often the practice of gaining consent is treated simply as a way of demonstrating the 'good practice' of the researcher. However, if it is meaningful, then the giving of consent and participation in the research is also a purposeful act by the research participant. Their choice to share their ideas and experiences with the researcher should be respected. In situations like the one described here, people are sharing their experience willingly, if not in conditions of their choosing (they might prefer, for example, not to have the kind of experiences that merit sharing in this way). Power inequalities are ever-present, but that does not mean that research participants, however vulnerable, should be treated as if they do not have their own agency and ability to make choices about sharing their lives – and, as in the example above, to question the situations in which they find themselves, including the research situation.

We are not able to provide any easy solutions to how researchers 'should' behave when such moments happen – except to suggest that they are important moments on which to reflect, when power relations are sharpened or perhaps shift slightly. To this end, we have provided below some questions for researchers or aspiring researchers to reflect on, which might help you to prepare for similar situations in your own fieldwork. You might find it helpful to discuss the questions below with others, particularly if they have different experiences of research (or life) from yours. You could also think together about why your responses are different or similar, share similar experiences you have encountered in research, and ask the same questions of those situations with hindsight.

How would you respond in the situation described in Emma's fieldnotes?

Try to imagine the situation and place yourself in it rather than thinking about what the 'right' response might be. What would your immediate reaction be? How might others present react, both to the initial situation and your response?

How far do you think your response relates to your own presentation of self, and the ways others might perceive you? Might your reactions be perceived differently if you were a researcher of a different gender, ethnicity, nationality, class? How might previous personal relationships (or their absence) affect your possible response?

Finally, what effect might your possible response in these situations have on the data you could collect? Would it produce different data in terms of responses from participants? Would your feelings about the situation make it into your analysis – explicitly or otherwise? How far do you think the interaction itself is important to analyse?

You may also find it useful to access an online video resource we have prepared based on another situation in our research, which raises similar questions. This can be found at https://youtu.be/ GbvwuXOVLHI.

References

Dreher, T. (2009) 'Eavesdropping with permission: The politics of listening for safer speaking spaces', *borderlands ejournal*, 8 (1), www. borderlands.net.au/vol8no1_2009/dreher_eavesdropping.htm [last accessed 22 May 2016].

Haraway, D. (1991) *Simians, Cyborgs and Women: The Reinvention of Nature*, London: Free Association Books.

Keith, M. (2005) *After the Cosmopolitan? Multicultural Cities and the Future of Racism*, London: Routledge.

Rose, G. (1997) 'Situating knowledges: Positionality, reflexivities and other tactics', *Progress in Human Geography*, 21 (3): 305–20.

5

Un/deserving migrants and resisting dehumanisation

Satwinder: Those that are good people should be given a visa and those who are bad people should be returned.
(Ealing and Hounslow focus group, conducted by Sukhwant)

Satwinder is someone who migrated to the UK, and who talked to us about the unfair treatment and prejudice she had received since doing so. Yet, her views seem close to the stance taken by the Immigration Minister Mark Harper, quoted in the opening to Chapter 2. Satwinder spoke about herself as having 'earned the right to live or settle in Britain', and others as less deserving of that right. The difference from Harper's 'rational' distinction (based on legal definition) is that here the distinction is being made on openly moral judgements of whether people are 'good' or 'bad'. For Satwinder there are those 'that are working' (good) and there are those that 'get caught up in drink and drugs and should not be here ... women drinking and smoking' (bad). A similar sentiment was echoed in a Bradford focus group by Nadia, an Iranian woman who had been settled in the UK for decades and now volunteers at a refugee and asylum seeker group. She said that perhaps it was good that the Go Home van scared some people:

Nadia: But I think sometime maybe it's good. Why I say that? I used to have a friend, and I haven't seen her for years, she was Asian, Pakistani, she married another Asian, it took them years to call them here to get married, marriage took only 3 days, he used her 3 days and after third days said, 'I only married to come to this country', and he just vanished. After 2 days they can't find him, so if for people like that I think it's good.
(Bradford Focus Group, conducted by Hannah)

Though Nadia's example might seem to be more closely concerned with the abuse of immigration rules than Satwinder's, both women emphasise morality rather than law: 'for people like that I think it's good'. What does it mean to draw such moral distinctions? What are the consequences? And how might we think about and understand the nature of such distinctions? In this chapter we will explore these questions by:

1   extending the ideas presented in Chapters 2 and 3 on how moral judgements form part of a 'postliberal' politics, by discussing how our research participants positioned themselves within discourses of antipathy to (illegal) immigration
2   showing how many people judged as 'bad migrants' seek to portray themselves as valuable citizens deserving of respect and protection. They do this by pointing to other individuals who behave badly, and who thereby constitute the 'real' problem
3   identifying ways in which people targeted by immigration control, and anti-racist and migrants' rights campaigners, have opened up debates about solidarity, belonging and deservingness in alternative and sometimes politically ambivalent ways
4   discussing how these perspectives have been used to develop forms of resistance to government anti-immigrant policies and rhetoric.

Devaluing migration

There has already been a great deal of academic analysis of the vilification of certain, usually impoverished, groups of migrants in the context of the austerity agenda (Hall, 2015), electoral politics (Forkert, 2014), differentiated citizenship, nationalism and exclusionary discourses of belonging (Balibar, 2004; Lentin and Titley, 2011; Mezzadra and Nielson, 2013). Our aim in this chapter, however, is not simply to identify discourses of demonisation but to understand better the local and personal consequences of such discourses and some of the (often rebellious or contradictory) reactions to them.

The work of the migration researcher Bridget Anderson (2013) and the sociologist Imogen Tyler (2013) has provided us with a theoretical context for understanding this situation – a situation in which sharp distinctions are drawn between insiders and outsiders, and where belonging will always be precarious and conditional. Each scholar provides considerable food for thought on the links between the devaluing and segmentation of migrants into 'deserving' and 'undeserving' and the scapegoating of other social groups, notably those existing at the margins of an ever-retracting welfare state:

benefits claimants, homeless people, single mums, sex workers and people with alcohol and drug dependency.

For Anderson, modern nation states are imagined as 'communities of value'. By this, she is referring not so much to 'British values'-type debates[1] but to the ways in which some citizens are seen to matter – to be of value – because of acting and existing in good and proper (valuable) ways. These 'good citizens' who are envisaged as 'law-abiding and hard-working members of stable and respectable families' (Anderson, 2013: 3) are then positioned by government, media and public discourses as being in need of external protection from Non-Citizens (foreigners and migrants) and internal protection from Failed Citizens ('benefit scroungers', paedophiles, rioters, criminals, etc.) (Anderson, 2013: 4). However, in reality, citizenship – even for the 'good citizen' – is not a natural and secured right: it is always a contingent relationship between a state and an individual, held open and differentiated along lines including race, class, gender, sexuality, disability and employment status (Anderson, 2013).

Anderson also argues that the recent waves of anti-immigrant hostility have relied on notions of a 'fantasy citizenship', in which new 'rights' – such as the 'right' to rent and the 'right' to work – have been named in public policy as if these actually mean something for national citizens (rather than being dependent on economic means, education and skills, or discrimination). According to Anderson (2015), the purpose has been to strengthen distinctions between those who hold national citizenship and those who do not. In other words, 'fantasy rights' conjured up by the state rely on the exclusion and demonisation of others. Moreover, this scapegoating operates within both neoliberal and postliberal frames which value (in a moral sense) those citizens who create exchange value. That is, those who are pro-ductive and aspirational (as good neoliberal subjects), and/or who fit conservative social norms of good behaviour (as good postliberal subjects), bearing in mind that even such behaviour may not be

---

[1] Claims to 'British values' have dominated debate about belonging and citizenship in Britain during the period of this study. They are often vague and disputed – particularly the idea that such values are exclusively British, or have been maintained historically or universally by Britain – but are defined, for example, in the guidelines for how such values must now be taught in schools, as values of 'democracy, the rule of law, indi-vidual liberty, and mutual respect for and tolerance of those with different faiths and beliefs and for those without faith' (Ofsted, 2015: 36; see also House of Lords Hansard, 2014).

enough given postliberal pessimism about cultural difference (see Chapter 3). Such framings have little use for those who are deemed economically unproductive or are seen to be unable to adapt to living in British society (learning English, etc.) – and they are often framed as a burden on limited resources. This is what Gavan Titley and Alana Lentin (2011) term 'good vs. bad diversity'. The bad migrant is located within a neoliberal frame that holds individuals (their morals, character and behaviour) responsible for poverty and inequality rather than structures and institutions (Rose, 1999). Social problems are passed off as the responsibility of individuals, and state intervention focuses on individual self-improvement and criminalisation rather than structural change.

It is important to note that these classifications are also highly gendered. Anderson's 'good citizen' combines the good behaviour expected of the modern liberal subject with traditional gender roles (the dutiful wife, the loving mother, the protective and providing husband – as we saw in Nadia's comments above, and Sara's reactions discussed in Chapter 1). At the same time the 'Non-Citizen' and the 'Failed Citizen' are depicted as uncivilised and parochial, epitomised by the caricature of the immigrant who has too many children in order to manipulate the welfare benefits system (Anderson, 2013: 7).

In her book *Revolting Subjects* (2013), Imogen Tyler identifies the affective and embodied dimensions of these characterisations of the modern state as reliant on the production of 'abject subjects' such as Travellers, asylum seekers and unemployed youth (2013: 4), who are identified as outsiders, so that others can be considered insiders. Tyler argues that, by producing disgust and repulsion towards a set of people who are made to seem abject ('revolting subjects'), governments encourage populations to align themselves as 'good citizens' against these 'revolting subjects', and thereby the limits of their own access to rights and citizenship are obscured. In developing these ideas, Tyler draws on the psychoanalytic concept of abjection, in particular Julia Kristeva's *Powers of Horror* (1982) – whereby the abject is a threat to meaning, identity and the social order, breaking down the distinction between self and other. A response to the abject is hatred and disgust. Kristeva had developed these ideas to understand xenophobia in *Strangers to Ourselves* (1991) as the 'prickly passions aroused by the intrusion of the "other" in the homogeneity of … a group' (Kristeva, 1991: 41). The 'other' then functions as a 'constitutive outside': people define their belonging by contrasting themselves with the 'other' or 'outsider' who does not belong. If we consider this in relation to postliberalism (as discussed in Chapter 3), this can help us understand the impulse of policy-makers to pay attention to these sorts of 'prickly passions' about immigration, rather than cold statistics about the benefits of immigration to the economy. The performance of coercion, as discussed in Chapter 2, is seen as an effective way of drawing attention to an outsider against whom people can define themselves, in order to feel more securely 'inside' the nation.

In the following discussion, we consider the ways in which some migrants and people from racially minoritised backgrounds responded to Home Office immigration campaigns by talking about and devaluing 'others' in order to legitimate their own presence. We explore how people who feel devalued may use and reinforce pre-existing social classifications and divisions in order to gain value and respectability for themselves, and legitimise their own claims to citizenship. In particular, we consider the manner in which they make use of distinctions between types of migrants or migration in their interactions with others in order to escape the kinds of disgust associated with groups maligned by dominant discourses.

Deserving citizenship and dis-identifying from the 'bad' migrant

A number of people we spoke to in the course of our research framed their own right to be in the UK (i.e. their sense of themselves as deserving citizens or good migrants) through recourse to narratives about work ethics and economic productivity:

> Kirsten: Do you feel that [your organisation] is affected by negative media coverage and if so how?
>
> Nader: Yeah, [our organisation] of course is affected by it because all the members – or most of them … are failed asylum seekers … The media ruined the reputation of asylum seekers in this country. They made the asylum seeker look like he is a criminal. Asylum seeker is not a crime … We are innocent people who came here to seek refuge. Just give us refuge. Give us our rights. Our rights is not money. We don't want money. We don't want support, we don't want housing. Give us the right of at least to work and I will support myself and all – I think most of the asylum seekers would do the same … I will work, I will rent, I will pay my contribution to the community, I will pay my tax, I will pay my rent, I will pay my Council Tax, I'll buy a car, I'll get a job, I'll be helpful for the community I'm living in. I will integrate.
>
> (Coventry Activist Interview, conducted by Kirsten)

Here Nader, an activist and an asylum seeker who was not allowed to work, was responding defensively to a news story in the *Coventry Telegraph* about the 2014 Immigration Bill (now law), and how immigration rhetoric and legislation position immigrants as not contributing to society. As part of this emphasis on 'making a contribution', he appeals for recognition and empathy on the basis of independence from state welfare. For example, when describing an encounter with a woman who believed that refugees were given free phones, cars etc., Nader emphasised that they were not in the UK for the welfare system:

> We are not here to seek support, we are here to seek asylum, we are here to seek refuge, a safe place to live, but we can depend on ourselves and contribute to the community and work and pay our contribution.
>
> (Coventry Activist Interview, conducted by Kirsten)

Some research participants used this 'model migrant' stereotype of hyper-productivity to validate themselves, but they also used it as a way of resisting a dominant narrative that derides 'illegal immigrants' as burdens on the taxpayer (Yukich, 2013). Neesha, quoted below, is a second-generation Indian woman who was defending 'illegal' immigrants as part of her wider rebuttal of the racism of Home Office immigration campaigns. However, her defence of 'illegal' immigrants relied on the characterisation of some white British people as lazy and dependent on benefits. Her comments contained expressions of disgust for the assumed characteristics of the 'benefit scrounger' (namely idleness, smoking, drinking and use of drugs):

> Neesha: White people don't work as hard as our own do ... I think the government are emphasising the fact that it's illegal but not the fact they [immigrants] are working. The message they should actually show is that this person is working, not that they are sitting at home, smoking god knows how many fags a day and drinking cans of beer and on drugs ... why don't they focus on the people who've been signing on and doing sweet 'F' anything for 20 years who say yes, I'm not gonna work because I'm better off on benefits? They are targeting people who are working, they may be illegal but they are working, they are contributing.
>
> (Ealing and Hounslow Focus Group, conducted by Sukhwant)

Neesha's reaction suggests the degree to which government immigration campaigns are inciting and exacerbating division, pitting excluded groups against each other. A defence of one excluded social group (the 'illegal immigrant') deploys moral judgements about the presumed lifestyles of other excluded groups (the benefit claimant). However, this is a dangerous position. Arguments about hard work, entrepreneurship and non-dependence on the state can also potentially play into the xenophobic charge that immigration is undercutting the 'white working class' by working in exploitative conditions that British people would not accept. This is the basis of many anti-immigration messages (e.g. Field, 2014) and was one mobilised to great effect during the 2016 EU referendum campaign.

'Good citizenship' is also seen to be embodied within certain behaviours, while other behaviours are seen as marking one as unfit for being a responsible citizen. Sometimes even smoking cigarettes and drinking alcohol could become potent signs of the undeserving citizen, and participants made assumptions about other people's immigration status solely on the basis of perceived 'bad behaviour', as Satwinder does here:

> There are a lot of men ... in the area that ... are paying money and coming here. And they are now in situations where they are taking drugs or alcohol. They are getting high and there are young women that are also getting into trouble or getting into bad ways. And this is a problem. So when people no longer have a visa, they should go.
> (Ealing and Hounslow Focus Group, conducted by Sukhwant)

As with other participants we have heard from in this chapter, Satwinder associated undeserving groups with criminality, illicit sex, theft and, in extreme cases, terrorism. Historically, these behaviours have been associated with people in vulnerable or dependent positions: 'racialised others, women, slaves, children, beggars, and those who were not able-bodied or those of "unsound mind" ' (Anderson 2013: 96). The good liberal citizen has also historically been framed in relation to a particular temperament, defined against the less desirable temperament of the migrant or the colonised other, who are often depicted as irrational, hot-tempered and superstitious. Such characterisations of temperament were also apparent within our focus group discussions where people who were seen as undeserving of the right to be in the UK were characterised as bad people not only in relation to a lack of productivity but also in relation to personality flaws, notably insincerity, manipulation, unreasonable behaviour and a bad temper.

Eastern Europeans were repeatedly singled out and characterised as being deceptive. For instance, Zimbabwean participants in a focus group in Glasgow described Eastern Europeans as 'naughty', 'stealing and fighting' and 'begging', and argued that 'they don't work' and are 'playing the system'. Some participants in the Bradford focus group of refugees and asylum seekers from around the world were anxious to know what had been said about them in the focus group with Eastern European migrants. Yet in the focus group with Eastern European migrants, the claims to respectability, and attempts to distance oneself from disrepute, were very similar:

> Hannah: I just wanted to ask what you think of that picture [of the Go Home van]?
>
> Lukas: Actually [what] they are saying is, they don't feel like illegal here now we are in the Eastern European, eastern Europe, and we are legal, can work, and …
>
> Hannah: Yes, no, and I'm not saying that that's – for you …
>
> Lukas: They say just that these people supposed to go home, who is stealing, making problems, who are not working … They are here for the work, to work, that's why they come here. She would do any job, she can't get job, she would do any job.
>
> (Bradford Focus Group, conducted by Hannah, English–Slovak interpreter (Lukas))

Through the interpreter, this group of mainly Slovakian nationals (and EU citizens) made clear that they were aware of their citizenship rights in the UK, and that the injunction to 'go home' could not now be legally applied to them. Nevertheless, they still felt their ability to be seen as part of the 'community of value' as somewhat tenuous. They insisted on their desire to work and provide for themselves; acting as 'guardians of good citizenship' (Anderson, 2013: 6), they contrasted themselves with others, 'who is stealing, making problems, who are not working'. Similarly, some of the women that participated in the Ealing and Hounslow focus groups (of South Asian, African and Caribbean origin), suggested that Eastern Europeans were benefit cheats. It seemed that for some participants, the simple act of accessing one's legal entitlement to welfare benefits could be construed as fraudulent behaviour.

As Bradford and Ealing and Hounslow activists noted, many of these distinctions settled on top of the unfinished business of historical and contemporary political tensions within local communities (see also Chapter 4). In particular, they pointed to existing schisms between Sikhs and Muslims, between Asians and newly arrived Roma communities, between Asians and Somalis. These communitarian schisms were criss-crossed by numerous nation and local dynamics. For example, there were also the divisive tactics of Muslim fundamentalist mobilisations on the one hand and of the government's 'war on terror' agenda on the other. These dynamics played out alongside racialised class politics which stirred up resentment among poor white communities by pointing to 'immigrants' in general as the reason for lack of jobs, housing or prospects, while long-term disinvestment in post-industrial areas such as Bradford, Coventry and elsewhere was ignored (see also Haylett, 2001).

We also heard how assumptions about migrants being morally unsound could be a part of institutional decisions. In the following extract, John, a Birmingham migrant rights advocate, talks about the culture of disbelief within the asylum system and social care responses to asylum seekers and refugees, by describing his struggle to get a mental health assessment for an Iranian asylum seeker who was suffering post-traumatic disorder due to experiencing torture and sexual abuse in prison:

> John: We were asking for a mental health assessment [of an asylum seeker] and Mental Health Services told him, without even having met the asylum seeker, that 'we'll meet with him but he's probably putting it on for his asylum claim'.
>
> (Birmingham Activist Interview, conducted by Kirsten)

The perception that asylum seekers are faking or exaggerating mental health problems in order to support their asylum claims, in line with media stereotypes of the 'bogus asylum seeker' (Smart et al., 2005; Thomas, 2012), has real consequences: a UK citizen with symptoms of mental distress is seen to be in genuine need, but the signs of pain or emotional distress for an asylum seeker are suspected of being fabricated.

You will now have a sense of the ways in which distinctions between migrants can be drawn in everyday conversations. However, we felt that it was not sufficient to conclude that people have simply internalised and are reproducing dominant messages about the untrustworthiness of (other) migrants, refugees or asylum seekers. One way of understanding what can be at work in these discourses is to consider them in relation to the sociologist Beverley Skeggs's work on value and respectability (1997, 2014). In particular, we think it worthwhile to consider Skeggs's exploration of the ways in which working-class women from the North-East of England attempted to distance themselves from their class by talking down other groups. Here is one of Skeggs's research participants talking about other working-class women:

> You know, you see them walking around town, dead fat, greasy hair, smelly clothes, dirty kids, you know the type, crimplene trousers and all, you know the type, I'd never be like that.
>
> (Therese, quoted in Skeggs, 1997: 83)

Such responses exist in a context where being working-class is seen both as shameful, especially when applied to women, 'as used to signify everything that is dirty, dangerous and without value' (Skeggs, 1997: 74) and as a form of judgement and categorisation, 'trying to fit people into pigeonholes' as one of her respondents put it (Skeggs, 1997: 77). The disparagement of others was a way in which the women could defend themselves from a dominant discourse that devalues them, and yet they could not entirely disconnect themselves from others because of the material reality of their class position.

Unsurprisingly, the claims for legitimacy we heard tended to be couched within the terms of the dominant discourse. Yet, because of the racialisation of discourses on immigration (see Chapter 6), the continued prevalence of racism and the material realities of the research participants' class positions, it was not necessarily possible for the people making these claims to escape the group identities that they appeared to be talking down. As we will discuss in the next section, a number of people we spoke to in the course of our research also pushed against these deserving/undeserving distinctions.

'Values beyond value'? Resisting anti-immigrant messaging

While some people we spoke with expressed their claims to belonging through appeals to individualised neoliberal values of productivity and aspiration, others resisted these values and reached instead for – to use Skeggs's phrase – 'values beyond (exchange) value' (2014). Seemingly banal comments about warmth, hospitality and love could be profound in a context where migrants were struggling against the daily strictures of immigration controls that are material, social and emotional. The following participants highlighted examples of everyday acts of kindness that had impacted positively on their own or other migrants' sense of self-worth, serving to resist or subvert dehumanisation:

Mary: And what I can say, it's a tough, very, very tough, asylum life here, it's horrible … but I'm lucky … I find warm and honest friend, British, in Birmingham … well I can say I like it, my city, and I love the British because they have honest people and good friend, very, very good friend, and look after me … I appreciate everything single one who support me, this city.

(Birmingham Focus Group, conducted by Kirsten)

Wendy: We've had other occasions where someone's arrived and have spoken hardly any English and neighbours … they bring them down to our organisation. They don't particularly want to get involved themselves but they just happen to know that we're there … and they turn up with them and say, 'We thought that they should know about your organisation.' So there are some marvellous acts of kindness actually.

(Bradford Activist Interview, conducted by Hannah)

Adam: There's one very interesting thing I find about Cardiff, you walk on the streets and people tell you 'good morning' in Cardiff … A woman told me 'good morning' this morning as well … It's good for you to be around good people. That someone to tell you 'good morning, good morning' it's good.

(Cardiff Focus Group, conducted by Roiyah)

In a sense these thoughts and experiences are part of an attempt to rehumanise social relations against a torrent of government interventions that are profoundly dehumanising. Some people went further than describing existing acts of kindness, to suggest that a wholly different type of politics was needed:

Mosef: If I was gonna change that [Go Home van] poster I'd have a poster saying love is the strongest emotion. Love don't fear.

(Cardiff Focus Group, conducted by Roiyah)

Lukas: He say it's no matter if you from Bangladesh, if you from India, or Czech Republic or Slovakia, with love! You can treat everything. You love somebody – or – treat somebody with love. It's completely different. There wouldn't be things like this.

(Bradford Focus Group, conducted by Hannah, English–Slovak interpreter (Lukas))

More practically perhaps, participants at the Glasgow focus group suggested that anti-immigrant sentiment could be tackled by, for instance, creating space for people to tell their stories and be heard by decision-makers, forcing politicians into more empathetic responses:

> Rose: I think if you can call that Theresa May, say to come down here [thumps table], we want to talk to her nicely, not badly, nicely.
> Immaculate: Or to ask her what do you think about people who left their families more than ten years ago …
> Rose: I would suggest you have the next plan maybe in the future, you publish this information, article, and public event, I would suggest would be better if you invite some maybe speaker or some other people to share their stories, quite important and very live for people, make a very big impact on people.
> (Glasgow Focus Group, conducted by Emma)

Other parts of the same focus group conversation provided insights into possible ways out of this all-pervading anti-immigrant rhetoric. These surfaced when some in the group wanted to distinguish themselves from the alcohol and drug users with whom they shared hostels and were challenged by another participant:

> Rose: I says to them, 'Please do something, put us in grades not to put asylum seekers together with the alcoholics, we are not like them, we don't do wrong to people, we are nice people.'
> Immaculate: Not just the drug addicts they are all just alcoholics.
> Rose: Both, drug addicts and alcoholics.
> (Glasgow Focus Group, conducted by Emma)

As with many of the examples discussed in the previous section, Rose and Immaculate seemed to judge the addictions of other residents, while simultaneously making a bid not to have their hard-fought-for asylum claims tarnished by the behaviour of other hostel residents. However, in response to this, Sirvan observed that passing moral judgements on other people's problems or circumstances involves validation of the same logic that informs Home Office anti-immigrant campaigns:

> Sirvan: See my understanding, if you make, say we are different with them, so that's the base of the things that they do, they said, 'We are better than you' … See if we do this it's discrimination, make you … that's why they do discrimination against us, they say 'we are better than you', if you say 'we are better than other people' that's the same principle.
> (Glasgow Focus Group, conducted by Emma)

For Sirvan, asylum seekers saying 'we are better than you' to addicts is a repetition of the same pattern of discrimination whereby asylum seekers and refugees are treated as lesser humans by others. Similarly, while discussing an image of the Go Home van, Grace problematised the distinctions being made by her peers between migrants arriving through different routes and with different visa statuses:

> Grace: Even some of my friends said that immigrants should 'go home'. They say 'I'm not talking about you, but let them go – the Eastern Europeans'. It's not like that, they can't say they're not talking about me, they are talking about me – we are all in the same boat, you can't just say 'you're okay' [and others are not].
> (Bradford Feedback Session, conducted by Hannah)

Echoing Martin Niemöller's famous poem 'First they came ...' (Niemöller, 1946), Grace argued that, if the Home Office started by targeting irregular migrants, they would soon come after others. She suggests the possibility of solidarity between different groups of people who are treated as a social problem, rather than the approach of seeking a more abject group against whom to define oneself as more deserving.

Interestingly, many participants emphasised the connection between generating alternative values and pro-immigrant protest. The starting point for some participants was a stand against apathy – the need for people to actually believe that they can change the terms of the debate. Within most of the focus groups, participants talked at some point about the need for local people to self-organise in order to defend the migrants in their area. For instance, while talking about the impact of the poster campaigns in Glasgow, Sirvan made the following point:

> we could stop this campaign ... encourage people to participate in the community and their organisation to fight for our rights.
> (Glasgow Focus Group, conducted by Emma)

In Bradford, on learning of the Go Home van for the first time, Aminata also suggested alternative direct action that might engage in – and shift – the terms of the performative politics of immigration control, by putting the ideas of home and belonging in question and erasing the illusion of a simplistic answer to immigration debates:

> Aminata: Yes, I said like these people doing it, their van, 'go home'. Like the Red Cross or the Refugee Council or World Health

Organisation, they can make their own van to protect the asylum seekers, to say, 'I don't have home'.

(Bradford Focus Group, conducted by Hannah)

The values base of pro-immigrant protest

During our research we observed many calls to action, street protests and demonstrations. These ranged from spur-of-the-moment activities to those involving detailed planning and preparation; from tactical engagements with the politics of performance to more traditional actions rooted in histories of labour and other liberation movements; and from those engaging with neoliberal logics of economics to post-liberal logics of morality, to those which suggested an alternative logic of social justice.

Alongside, and linked to, these on-the-ground activities, at a national level, the Joint Council for the Welfare of Immigrants and Movement Against Xenophobia's '#IAmAnImmigrant' campaign brought together myth-busting information and individual testimonies in the runup to the 2015 General Election (see also Chapter 6). The campaign comprised photographs of fifteen people introducing themselves and the contribution they had made to society, and declaring themselves to be immigrants, displayed on 440 billboards across the London Underground and another 550 at railway stations across the country. The popularity of the campaign was demonstrated by the fact that over £50,000 was raised through crowd funding within a matter of weeks to fund this public advertising. Thousands of people have now used the hashtag to share photographs of these posters, which carry short testimonies of people who at some point migrated to the UK and have been involved in improving the quality of others' lives – a nurse, a fireman, a teacher and a lawyer are among those depicted. In addition, many members of the public have taken up the invitation to add their own story to their website in a similar format.[2] In putting a 'human face' to the figure of the immigrant, this campaign has been seen as important for rehumanising the debate about migration and emphasising the contributions being made by migrants in relation to the economy but also in relation to civil society and social welfare.

We would also suggest that there are limits to how far such a framing challenges the underlying logic of a distinction between good

---

[2] See www.iamanimmigrant.net/my-story.

and bad migrants, or deserving and undeserving citizens that we have discussed in this chapter. It figures the poster boys and girls of the campaign as human and relatable (see Chapter 6), but on the basis of their contribution to society, rather than their existence as fellow human beings. Nevertheless, it is a pragmatic response to the performative politics of stigmatisation, using the same tools of performance to attempt to create a (post?)-political space in which the consensus that might be reached is one about the human face of 'the immigrant'.

Elsewhere, we have seen that while the Westminster postliberal consensus has seemingly rejected the neoliberal idea that the economic contribution of individual migrants has any weight in political debate (see Chapter 3), there are ways in which campaigns based on economic arguments have influenced aspects of the 'hostile environment'. Hot on the heels of the decision not to extend Operation Vaken, there was stiff opposition to the coalition government's 2013 proposal to introduce £3,000 'visa bonds' for applications by those entering the UK from six specific countries – India, Pakistan, Bangladesh, Sri Lanka, Nigeria and Ghana – identified as at 'high risk' of overstaying their visa. Jasjit, an activist in Ealing and Hounslow (interviewed by Sukhwant), explained that these proposals were dropped because a number of government departments – including the Foreign and Commonwealth Office, the Department for Business, Innovation and Skills and the Department for Communities and Local Government – expressed their opposition, and the then Deputy Prime Minister Nick Clegg threatened to veto the plans. Politicians who had otherwise been silent on the development of the Home Secretary's 'hostile environment' raised concerns about the implications for a government courting trade relations with India and Nigeria. While the attempt to discuss migrant contributions to the national economy have lost favour in political debate, within diplomatic circles it still seems that money talks.

In more on-the-ground political protests, some of our participants had themselves been involved in demonstrations. In response to an image of people opposing the poster campaign in Glasgow, Immaculate noted that people subject to immigration rules are at the forefront of protests against the government's communications:

> Immaculate: At the moment there's a group of asylum seekers and refugees they're actually going to the Home Office campaigning in front every week, they have just decided they're not any organisation to support them, they're doing it on their own, they are doing it every week now, and they said they won't stop. They will

be there every week in front of the Home Office, whether it's one
or two turn up, they are going to do every week.

(Glasgow Focus Group, conducted by Emma)

Manoj, a London activist who works for an anti-racist advocacy
project (interviewed by Sukhwant), described how the contributions of immigrants to the economy were made visible in a more
oppositional and grassroots-led way, in the community resistance of
2013 that came to be known as 'the Chinatown shutdown'. After
Home Office Enforcement teams increased the intensity of their
'fishing raids' looking for migrants working illegally in businesses in
London's Chinatown, concerns were raised about both the racial
profiling of the Chinese community and the impact on Chinese businesses. This gave rise to a broad-based resistance that included businesses, anti-racists and cultural organisations, whereby staff in
restaurants throughout Chinatown closed their businesses and took
to the streets to protest about the heavy-handed immigration raids,
on 22 October 2013.

Other activists sought to reorient the discussion to address those
issues that are veiled by anti-immigrant rhetoric because, as the political scientist Shamit Saggar (2004) has argued, immigration is often
a proxy for other concerns. As discussed in previous chapters (see
especially Chapter 2), we held a focus group in Dagenham with
people who identified themselves as British National Party (BNP)
supporters. Their discussion suggests how immigration becomes the
empty signifier into which people pour a range of concerns and complaints, such as those relating to housing needs, cuts to the National
Health Service, health and social care, local authority accountability
and the contracting out of local council services. Notably these were
all concerns about the distribution and management of public goods.
Moreover, it was clear from the speakers at a September 2013 demonstration outside the Glasgow reporting centre (Emma's fieldnotes),
that focusing political resistance back on to jobs, housing and health
has been an important angle for counter-mobilisations. This was also
the cornerstone of the response by Gary, a leading trade union activist
in London, who argued that counter-messaging should focus on
getting behind the immigration façade and focusing on those other
concerns:

Gary: We're trying to come up with a project which looks at trying
to change the nature of the debate that we have around migration
to focus instead on, if you like, shifting the blame. So migrants
are getting blamed for various things and people see migrants as

a problem. So what you do is try and come up with ways of shifting the blame for migration from migrants to other people … [For example] it's not the fault of migrants that there are these problems. It's the fault of employers. Because what employers are doing is using migrants to exploit their labour. It's not the fault of migrants because there's problems about access to local services, for two reasons. One, migrants are providing local services and it's easy to find [evidence for that]. And secondly … services are under pressure because they're getting cut … Because from our perspective, migration is a proxy issue. Yeah, there's a level of racism there and xenophobia but the real concern about people when you hear them talk about migration is they don't just talk about immigrants, they talk about immigrants in relation to getting jobs, getting access to services, getting housing.
(London Activist Interview, conducted by Sukhwant)

Gary suggested that solidarities between newly arrived migrants and racially minoritised citizens who are settled in Britain will inevitably arise because the latter will be affected by the same 'hostile environment', as landlords and employers decide to 'play it safe' by discriminating against non-white applicants to avoid falling foul of the Immigration Act 2014 and Immigration Bill 2015–16, which make private landlords liable for checking the visa or settlement status of their tenants. However, he argued that, beyond this coincidence of concerns, solidarities need to be actively mobilised and produced by identifying shared experiences of exploitation and material conditions across racial divides.

Gary: At the moment, what you have is very similar kinds of exploitation but this barrier that comes down … well yeah, you're getting exploited but that's fine because you're a migrant, I'm getting exploited but that's not okay because I'm a Brit … One of the potentials for me is … to [show] people that their stories are very similar.
(London Activist Interview, conducted by Sukhwant)

Gary argues for changing the conversation from one that continues to be located within the neoliberal frame of productivity to one that counters anti-immigrant sentiment from an anti-racist and socialist perspective. Others recognised the value of revisiting histories of racism and colonialism to revive historical solidarities, particularly within local areas where anti-racist mobilisations have been linked to a defence of immigration and public welfare services (see also Chapter 4).

Participants in many of our focus groups made connections between the treatment of asylum seekers and the legacy of colonialism, particularly the double standards in terms of the presence and treatment of British people in other countries, as compared to the hostility faced in the UK:

> Parveena: I'm from India, they ruled my country for 250 years, and they have taken everything. I wouldn't say that all our population are coming here, people who are in need are coming here, then why don't they give the hospitality for the people?
> (Birmingham Focus Group, conducted by Kirsten)

> Amadou: In other parts of the world, in the foreign countries if these people or any foreign people come, they respect them. And they treat them more than as a guest.
> Mohammed: Why don't they treat us the same?
> (Birmingham Focus Group, conducted by Kirsten)

When participants conceptualised issues in these ways, it seemed to us that they were moving beyond either the neoliberal (economic) or postliberal (moralistic) framing of immigration. In a way they were politicising and historicising the valuing of warmth, hospitality and love described earlier by Mary, Wendy, Adam, Mosef and others. If there is a moralistic element to this politics, it is not the call to 'respectability' of postliberalism but a call for fairness and justice, for taking into account the historical injustices of colonialism and capitalism that have led to the current geopolitics of migration.

As with the women who came together at Southall Black Sisters to protest against immigration enforcement raids (see Chapter 4), it was clear from the local area studies that voluntary-sector contexts, or simply spaces to discuss these issues, could facilitate the ability to think of 'values beyond [exchange] value', to return to Skeggs's term, and build networks of solidarity that could help to translate these values into action, and counter the tendency to pit groups of people against each other.

Conclusion

In this chapter we have argued for the importance of contextualising narratives of deservingness by situating them within wider social settings. Our findings suggest that, as migration is devalued, claims to economic productivity are increasingly used to validate citizenship and to talk down other groups, so that work, aspiration, productivity and conformity with socially conservative behaviour codes have increasingly become proxies for nationalism, rights and belonging. In addition, the recourse to a fantasy citizenship based on a continually recalibrated array of distinctions and entitlements is a way of negotiating and often sidestepping existing differentiation in citizenship on the basis of race, gender, sexuality, disability and class.

Our research has also shown that anti-immigration messages from government and the media are not simply internalised. Some of the people we interviewed resisted anti-immigration messaging by countering the imperative for people to pit themselves against each other on the basis of their immigration status or nationality. The organisations they belonged to often created the space for these discussions to take place. Most importantly, recoupling debates on racism and immigration control seemed to help to challenge distinctions between deserving and undeserving migrants, as in the connections between colonial histories and the current geopolitics of migration control drawn by Parveena, Amadou and Mohammed. Protest actions both real (the SBS street protest, the Chinatown Shutdown, #IAmAnImmigrant) and imagined (the 'I don't have a home' van Aminata describes, the 'fight for our rights' Sirvan imagines) can help create solidarity across national, ethnic and class lines. The appeal to recognition of the worthwhile character of (some) migrants as productive neoliberal subjects of the #IAmAnImmigrant campaign contrasted with the more traditional trade-union-inspired politics of a withdrawal of labour and demonstration of power in the Chinatown Shutdown. Yet both can be seen as attempts to counter the postpolitical and postliberal politics of immigration control (see Chapters 2 and 3) with alternative performances. Coupled with the attempts to refigure discussions to recognise colonial and labour histories, as many of our participants described and attempted, this has the potential to be a powerful antidote to the performances of toughness, threat and exclusion which currently dominate public debates on immigration and its control. The increasingly controversial nature of such debates shows the importance of both creating networks of solidarity and articulating such alternative values – and as publicly as possible.

References

Anderson, B. (2013) *Us and Them? The Dangerous Politics of Immigration Control*, Oxford: Oxford University Press.

Anderson, B. (2015) Keynote at *Mapping Immigration Controversies* conference, University of Warwick, 10 June, www.youtube.com/watch?v=nNPMKZRhvgo [last accessed 22 May 2016].

Balibar, E. (2004) *We, the People of Europe? Reflections on Transnational Citizenship*, Princeton: Princeton University Press.

Field, F. (2014) 'The lower classes have serious, and justifiable concerns about mass immigration', *The Spectator*, 8 July, http://blogs.spectator.co.uk/2014/07/the-government-must-address-the-effect-of-mass-immigration-on-poorer-voters/ [last accessed 22 May 2016].

Forkert, K. (2014) 'Who's being ignored when politicians are claiming they are listening to concerns about immigration?', *Mapping Immigration Controversy*, 2 December, http://mappingimmigrationcontroversy.com/2014/12/02/whos-being-ignored-when-politicians-claim-they-are-listening-to-concerns-about-immigration/ [last accessed 22 May 2016].

Hall, S. (2015) 'Focus: Migration and election 2015', *Discover Society*, 17, 1 February, http://discoversociety.org/2015/02/01/focus-migration-and-election-2015/ [last accessed 22 May 2016].

Haylett, C. (2001) 'Illegitimate subjects?: Abject whites, neoliberal modernisation, and middle-class multiculturalism', *Environment and Planning D: Society and Space*, 19(3): 351–70.

House of Lords Hansard (2014) 'Schools: British Values', 754, 12 June, https://hansard.parliament.uk/Lords/2014-06-12/debates/14061243000356/SchoolsBritishValues [last accessed 22 May 2016].

Kristeva, J. (1982) *Powers of Horror: An Essay on Abjection*, trans. L.S. Roudiez, New York: Columbia University Press.

Kristeva, J. (1991) *Strangers to Ourselves*, trans. L.S. Roudiez, New York: Harvester Wheatsheaf.

Lentin, A. and Titley, G. (2011) *The Crises of Multiculturalism: Racism in a Neoliberal Age*, London: Zed Books.

Mezzadra, S. and Nielson, B. (2013) *Border as Method: or the Multiplication of Labour*, Durham, NC: Duke University Press.

Niemöller, M. (1946) 'First they came for the socialists …'. For full text see *United States Holocaust Memorial Museum*: www.ushmm.org/wlc/en/article.php?ModuleId=10007392 [last accessed 19 June 2016].

Ofsted [Office for Standards in Education] (2015) *School Inspection Handbook: Handbook for Inspecting Schools in England under Section 5 of the Education Act 2005*, Manchester: Ofsted, www.gov.uk/government/publications/school-inspection-handbook-from-september-2015 [last accessed 19 June 2016].

Rose, N. (1999) *Powers of Freedom: Reframing Political Thought*, Cambridge: Cambridge University Press.

Saggar, S. (2004) 'Immigration and the politics of public opinion', *The Political Quarterly*, 74 (s1): 178–94.

Skeggs, B. (1997) *Formations of Class and Gender: Becoming Respectable*, London: Sage.

Skeggs, B. (2014) 'Values beyond value: Is there anything beyond the logic of capital?', *British Journal of Sociology*, 65 (1): 1–20.

Smart, K., Grimshaw, R., McDowell, C. and Crosland, B. (2005) *Reporting Asylum: The UK Press and the Effectiveness of PCC Guidelines*, London: ICAR, http://www.crimeandjustice.org.uk/sites/crimeandjustice.org.uk/files/ReportingAsylum.pdf [last accessed 22 May 2016].

Thomas, A. (2012) 'Asylum seekers continue to be stigmatised by the British press', *The Guardian*, 31 October, www.theguardian.com/media/2012/oct/31/asylum-seekers-stigmatised-british-press [last accessed 22 May 2016].

Tyler, I. (2013) *Revolting Subjects: Social Abjection and Resistance in Neoliberal Britain*, London: Zed Books.

Yukich, G. (2013) 'Constructing the model immigrant', *Social Problems*, 60 (3): 302–20.

Living Research Five: Public anger in research (and social media)

At our end-of-project conference, one participant said that the event had made her think that 'when outraged by something' she would try to research it; 'combine activism with academia and your sociological imagination'. Strikingly, this comment captured much of what brought us together to develop the research discussed in this book. In this section, we will tell a story of how sparks of outrage and anger led to this research, consider how social media allowed us to connect and channel that anger, reflect on the ways in which we tried to use these emotions and technologies in the process of our research and identify some of the findings from engaging with social media as a research tool.

Twitter and anger as motivators

When the Home Office launched Operation Vaken in July 2013 (see Chapter 1) all of the authors of this book were angered by the seeming overt and unapologetic racism of the Go Home van slogan, apparent racial profiling in immigration checks in public places and the Home Office's publication of images of raids through Twitter using the #immigrationoffenders hashtag (see Figure 3). We expressed this over email, on social media and in conversation. Several weeks earlier, some of us, with others, had met as a group of academics and activists when Gargi organised a workshop on 'race critical public scholarship' at the University of East London (for a sense of the discussions there, see Murji and Bhattacharyya, 2013). Drawing on links we had established there and elsewhere, and using a combination of online and offline communications, we came together as a research team in response to developing Home Office initiatives, as described in Chapter 1.

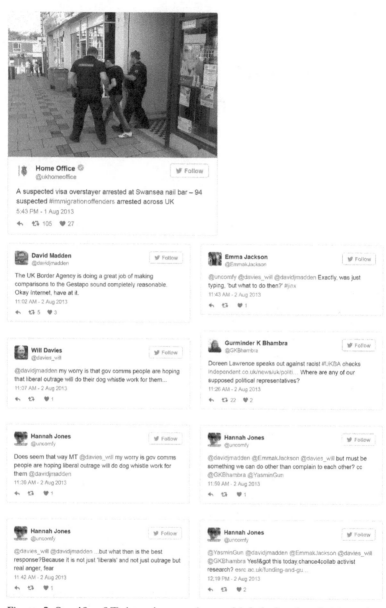

Figure 3: Storify of Twitter interactions which helped to initiate the research for this book

We managed – at least by the standards of academic research! – to act quickly to gather networks, plan and begin the project. This was aided by communication tools like Twitter (see Figure 3), in conjunction with 'in-person' relationships between colleagues, friends and collaborators. We were motivated to do this research by a mutual commitment to 'public sociology' (Burawoy, 2005) – that is, a belief in the importance of bringing sociological analysis of people, power and institutions to a public audience for use in understanding everyday questions, struggles and situations. We worked as a group because this made the most sense in terms of pooling ideas, expertise and resources and learning. We also tried to maintain dialogue beyond the research team throughout each stage of the research – including with wider publics through Twitter, blogs, public meetings and media engagement (see also Living Research Three and Six).

It might seem odd to suggest that research – never mind collaborative, publicly engaged research – could be motivated by anger. Anger is often viewed as a negative emotion – either as destructive or as distracting from calm analysis or action. However, the writer and activist Audre Lorde has written powerfully of the value of anger as a motivator:

> Every woman has a well-stocked arsenal of anger potentially useful against those oppressions, personal and institutional, which brought that anger into being. Focused with precision it can become a powerful source of energy serving progress and change. And when I speak of change, I do not mean a simple switch of positions or a temporary lessening of tensions, nor the ability to smile or feel good. *I am speaking of a basic and radical alteration in those assumptions underlining our lives* ... anger expressed and translated into action in the service of our vision and our future is a liberating and strengthening act of clarification.
>
> (Lorde, 1984; emphasis added)

Lorde is here talking about anger and passion in motivating activism and political change. As academic researchers, our role might be more readily imagined as *finding out* and *analysing* rather than *changing* things. However, in the lines emphasised in the above quote, Lorde speaks of change as 'a basic and radical alteration in ... assumptions'. Part of social research must always be about gathering evidence that helps to demonstrate contradictions in common-sense assumptions, and producing new ways of thinking that help us understand those assumptions and their contradictions – and perhaps thereby change things. The power of anger as a motivating force, as Lorde argues and as our research here demonstrates, does not necessarily remove space for analytical and careful thought, but instead can point us to areas where such thought is urgently needed (see Chapter 1 for a discussion of how this relates to ideas about 'militant investigation' (Casas-Cortes et al., 2014) in migration research).

Anger and activism on Twitter

We built analysis of social media into our research – since the Home Office had used them in its own campaigns, but also as an increasingly important format for political debate, and a medium whose role in political activism has not yet been fully understood. We wanted to see how people used Twitter to respond to Home Office campaigns, not just in terms of the content of what they said but also the ways in which this use interacted with other forms of response. If people were angry, did they let off steam with a tweet and then forget it, as Jodi Dean suggests in *Blog Theory*? Dean asks whether social media constitute 'communication for its own sake', and cautions that 'the affective charges we transmit and confront reinforce and extend affective networks without encouraging – and, indeed, by displacing – their consolidation into organized political networks' (2010: 119). That is, Dean suggests that interactions on social media do not go beyond sharing humour or outrage. But we wanted to ask whether, in sharing through this medium, possibilities were created for 'anger expressed and translated into action', as Audre Lorde might imagine.

One method we tried out as part of our online ethnography was to organise Twitter debates using the project's @MICResearch Twitter account, asking our Twitter followers provocative questions which we hoped would open up debate. While there were a few interesting exchanges, overall there was not much discussion. We found, perhaps unsurprisingly, that the more dynamic engagements and online conversations emerged organically in response to our project tweets and blog posts, and especially during our workshops and conference, rather than through deliberately orchestrated online discussions. Perhaps this points to the need to engage with social media through its own logic – to understand its flows of discussion and meaning organically, rather than something that can be engineered through tools more suited to other forms of interaction, such as focus groups. Importantly, we recognised that the 'organic' ways in which Twitter worked to develop discussion and action was not simply in an online forum, but through the interactions between 'real-life' events and engagements, and online ones.

Many responses to the Home Office both politically and playfully highlighted the heavy-handedness of their campaign – at the same time increasing its reach as a news story and topic of public debate. Some responses demonstrated the absurdity of the government campaign by taking it at its word. The Twitter user Pukkah Punjabi wrote about how she had called the number advertised and asked for help to go home – to her home in Willesden Green, North London (Punjabi, 2013). Hundreds of people followed suit (asking to be sent back to Scotland, the West Country and East London for example), and the Home Office's own evaluation of Operation Vaken found that 1,034 (66 per cent) of the texts and 13 (14 per cent) of the calls received in response to the van were classified as 'hoax'; added to this, 123 (8 per cent) of the texts and 21 (23 per cent) of the calls they received were complaints (Home Office, 2013). Though apparently minor acts of protest – and perhaps in some cases simply jokes – it seems to us that these responses managed to respond nimbly, turning the government's own choice of communication method back on itself, jamming the signal, within the tradition of 'culture jamming'.[1]

The image of the Go Home van, like the #racistvan hashtag, became a meme which long outlasted the summer of 2013. The civil rights organisation Liberty produced its own (real-life) van with the slogan 'Stirring up tension and division in the UK illegally? Home Office, think again,' targeted at gaining press and social media attention. More informally, photoshopped parodies multiplied on Twitter; examples included a slogan telling the Romans to go home (playing on the Monty Python 'what did the Romans ever do for us?' joke); another told the Australian lobbyist Lynton Crosby (rumoured to be behind the idea of the Go Home van) to go home, pointing out the irony of an Australian telling immigrants to leave the UK. Later, Mark Harper MP (Immigration Minister at the time of Operation Vaken) was caught employing a cleaner whose visa was not in order and forced to resign, and so his face ended up on the side of a photoshopped van too. The Go Home van reappeared as a satirical template in the run up to the May 2014 European Parliament

---

[1]The term 'culture jamming' was coined in 1984 by Don Joyce of the experimental music band Negativland, and since then has become more widely used to mean the appropriation and subversion of media representations. See Chandler and Neumark (2005).

election, this time with the anti-EU and anti-immigration UK Independence Party (UKIP) more often than not the target of the joke.

Twitter was used also as a means of organising on-the-ground resistance to immigration raids. Where the Home Office had tried to disseminate news of its success in numbers of arrests during raids, activists shared sightings of (increasingly visible) Immigration Enforcement vehicles and officers on streets around the UK. Sometimes this was through organised activist groups like the Anti-Raids Network and London Black Revolutionaries, in other cases individual Twitter users shared the locations of their sightings. In some cases, this simply alerted others that raids were taking place; in others, it seems to have enabled activists to arrive on the scene and disrupt enforcement actions. This use of social media, not just to raise awareness but to organise and co-ordinate direct action in person, suggests that its role in the political arena should not simply be dismissed as 'clicktivism' – the idea that political action is reduced simply to the click of a mouse, without further engagement. As the journalist Laurie Penny said after the 2015 General Election, 'an angry population is hard to govern; a depressed population is easy' (2015). Anger can also provoke us to act, as was the case for us and our project. Online platforms present both possibilities and limitations in terms of how anger and humour can be used to mobilise or to create dialogue, within and beyond research.

If you conduct social research yourself, what motivates you to do it? If you read or use social research, what motivates you to do so?

What do you think is the place of anger, or other emotions, in social research? How would you reconcile the idea of research motivated by anger with ideas of scientific objectivity or ideas of situated subjects (see also Living Research Four)?

Do you use social media such as Twitter? If so, what do you use it for? Do you see it as a tool of the social researcher? What are the challenges and limitations of using social media as:

1   a source of already-existing data to analyse
2   a method or tool for producing new data
3   a tool for disseminating research findings?

References

Burawoy, M. (2005) 'For public sociology', *American Sociological Review*, 70: 4–28.

Casas-Cortes, M., Cobarrubias, S., De Genova, N., Garelli, G., Grappi, G., Heller, C., Hess, S., Kasparek, B., Mezzadra, S., Neilson, B., Peano, I., Pezzani, L., Pickles, J., Rahola, F., Riedner, L., Scheel, S. and Tazzioli, M. (2014) 'New keywords: migration and borders', *Cultural Studies*, 29 (1): 1–33.

Chandler, A. and Neumark, N. (eds) (2005) *At a Distance: Precursors to Art and Activism on the Internet*, Cambridge, MA: MIT Press.

Dean, J. (2010) *Blog Theory: Feedback and Capture in the Circuits of Drive*, Cambridge: Polity.

Home Office (2013) *Operation Vaken Evaluation Report October 2013*, London: Home Office, https://www.gov.uk/government/uploads/ system/uploads/attachment_data/file/254411/Operation_ Vaken_Evaluation_Report.pdf [last accessed 22 May 2016].

Lorde, A. (1984) *Sister Outsider: Essays and Speeches*, Freedom, CA: The Crossing Press.

Murji, K. and Bhattacharyya, G. (eds) (2013) *Race Critical Public Scholarship (Ethnic and Racial Studies*, London: Routledge.

Penny, L. (2015) 'Don't give in: An angry population is hard to govern; a depressed population is easy', *New Statesman*, 9 May, http:// www.newstatesman.com/politics/2015/05/dont-give-angry-population-hard-govern-depressed-population-easy [last accessed 22 May 2016].

Punjabi, P. (2013) 'The day I asked the Home Office to help me go home – to Willesden Green', *The Guardian*, 28 July, www. theguardian.com/commentisfree/2013/jul/28/willesden-green-twitter-wind-up-immigrants [last accessed 22 May 2016].

6

Conclusion: 'Ordinary' people and immigration politics

We construct borders, literally and figuratively, to fortify our sense of who we are; and we cross them in search of who we might become. They are philosophies of space, credibility contests, latitudes of neurosis, signatures to the social contract, soothing containments, scars.

(Frances Stonor Saunders, 2016: 8)

In January 2001, with the Twin Towers still standing, Lehman Brothers still trading and Blairism at its most popular, the UK government's Cabinet Office published a paper, 'Migration: An Economic and Social Analysis' (Cabinet Office, 2001). Reviewing various sources of economic evidence on migration, the general thrust of the analysis was unambiguous: immigration is economically beneficial. It opened with a bullishly liberal quotation from Tony Blair at Davos the previous year, 'we have the chance in this century to achieve an open world, an open economy, and an open global society with unprecedented opportunities for people and business' (Blair, 2000). The Cabinet Office report itself found that 'migration is likely to enhance economic growth and the welfare of both migrants and natives ... There is little evidence that native workers are harmed by immigration ... [and] The broader fiscal impact of migration is likely to be positive' (2001: 5–7).

The journey from that historical moment of seemingly free market cosmopolitanism to the Go Home vans of 2013 and the subsequent EU referendum decision in 2016 for Britain to leave the European Union, in part as a response to fears about immigration (see Chapter 1 for the connections between the referendum and anti-immigration discourses), is one shaped by a number of diverse forces, events and conditions. In the early 2000s, real wage growth slowed dramatically, before turning negative in early 2007, heralding the start of the global financial crisis (Machin, 2015). Following global upheavals including civil war in Sierra Leone, land reform and economic collapse in

Zimbabwe, and the NATO invasion of Afghanistan, asylum applications in Britain reached a peak. They were at their highest with 84,130 applications (excluding dependents) in 2002 (up from 4,256 in 1987; the 2014 figure was 24,914) (Blinder, 2015). As the number of asylum applications grew, a system of dispersal was put in place from 1999, with asylum seekers temporarily housed in centres around the UK, to 'ease the pressure' on housing and services in London and south-east England. This meant that many cities, such as Glasgow and Cardiff, saw a large number of new arrivals from around the world, and in a relatively short period of time. The 2004 enlargement of the EU, plus the UK's decision not to restrict access to citizenship for the new entrants, greatly increased the levels of immigration from within the EU (Vargas-Silva and Markaki, 2015).

In the first decade of the twenty-first century, British political debate in Britain led by Tony Blair as Prime Minister focused on 'good' economic migration (people coming to the UK to bring skills and increase national wealth). This focus was sharpened by the simultaneous demonising of 'bogus asylum seekers' as an illegitimate burden on public services and a risk to a cohesive and peaceful society (Back et al., 2002; Home Office, 2002). Although there has been some reduction in the use of demeaning epithets such as 'illegal asylum seeker' and 'bogus asylum seeker' in public discourses – following guidance from the Press Complaints Commission in 2003[1] – the idea of illegitimate migrations remains (see Chapter 1). Although the heightened visibility of the European 'crisis' of migration since 2015 has led to prefacing of some anti-immigration rhetoric with an emphasis on a historical imagining of Britain as always offering welcome to people fleeing persecution, this sits alongside the effort to create and portray a palpably hostile environment for certain migrants in ways that we have explored throughout the book.

Within this hostile environment there remains recognition that immigration touches all of our lives, as world populations are increasingly on the move, and where this movement is full of historical and geo-social layerings and legacies of transit and encounter. Politicians' calls to 'ordinary people' who are affected by immigration control are often imagined as summoning an audience that is sedentary, racially 'pure' and 'at home', but affected by the migrant 'other'. However, even as migration for better opportunities, for family reunion and in search of safety are each deemed suspect or threatening, we also see

---

[1] Because it cannot be illegal to seek asylum, although asylum may not be granted.

a fracturing of populist posturing on immigration. At times a sense of common humanity breaks through, so that even those crossing borders outside of designated and orderly channels can be perceived as 'ordinary people'. Here, there is perhaps an opportunity to shift the terms and register of the conversation.

Throughout this book we have discussed the ways that British government communications about immigration control have crept into everyday, ordinary lives. Sometimes this is in a manner that jolts people out of complacency. The Go Home van is one example. This initiative seemingly planned to be high-profile and provocative, reassuring certain sections of the public that the government was taking action, not only raised public concerns about immigration numbers, it also incited questions about whether immigration enforcement itself was 'out of control'. Sometimes the communications are less spectacular, a banal seeping into local and national news reports of the numbers of 'immigration offenders' apprehended from their homes, workplaces or weddings; perhaps a visible presence of officers and vehicles on the lookout for offenders, telling us that irregular migrants are everywhere and enforcement officers are ready to pounce on those who seem suspicious. We have drawn on our research with people in England, Scotland and Wales to consider what the consequences might be of these everyday prompts that associate certain forms of migration with suspicion and unlawfulness, for people who are worried about migration as a threat, for people who feel under suspicion and for those who reject this idea and want to embrace migration as both valuable and inevitable. In these concluding thoughts, we will draw together some of the themes outlined in the book by:

1   reflecting on what our findings mean for 'ordinary people', and what is meant by 'ordinary people' in different contexts
2   discussing how immigration politics is entangled with questions of race and racism
3   considering some of the lessons we have learnt in writing the book, and how the book might be useful for others.

Who is ordinary?

For too long, the benefits of immigration went to employers who wanted an easy supply of cheap labour; or to *the wealthy metropolitan elite* who wanted cheap tradesmen and services – but not to the *ordinary, hard-working people* of this country.

(Brokenshire, 2014: 8; emphasis added)

In this speech by the then Immigration Minister, James Brokenshire, to the Demos think tank in 2014, we hear a refrain that has echoed throughout the book in how concerns about immigration itself (particularly in terms of the numbers of new arrivals and people breaking immigration rules) are characterised as the worries of 'ordinary people'. This appeal to 'ordinary people' is in contrast to concerns that immigration control is too harsh, a view often allied with a 'liberal metropolitan elite'. It is worth stopping to ask where these characterisations come from, and what purpose they serve, as well as asking what truth there is to them.

In *Keywords* (1976), Raymond Williams complicates the use of the term 'ordinary' by examining its etymology, which originally denoted something mandated by rule (with the same roots as 'ordinance'). The word has come to mean 'something done by custom', but has also taken on a negative sense, with connotations of inferiority (e.g. 'very ordinary looking') (p. 225):

> Thus 'ordinary people' can be used to express a social attitude or prejudice in effectively opposite ways. 'What ordinary people believe' can, in different contexts, mean either what 'uneducated' … people know or think, in what are then clearly seen as limited ways, or what 'sensible', 'regular', 'decent' people believe, as distinct from the views of some sect, or of intellectuals.
>
> (Williams, 1976: 225–6)

This is a very clear description of how 'ordinary people' are named and centred in immigration debates. In Brokenshire's speech above, for example, we can see the political rhetoric that connects with the shifting policy tendencies outlined in Chapter 2. When the tendency shifts from a neoliberal to a 'postliberal' approach, it follows that former neoliberal approaches are blamed for favouring economic measures over social ones. A populist call is made to 'ordinary, hard-working people' (and who, after all, does not see themselves as ordinary and hard-working?). It is posited that problems in the economy and elsewhere that affect ordinary people are associated with immigration; that ordinary people will be listened to and those problems addressed. This same logic emerged with the results of the EU referendum in June 2016, when UKIP's leader Nigel Farage declared that the result was a 'victory for real people, a victory for ordinary people, a victory for decent people' (Asthana et al., 2016).

Certainly, some of the people we interviewed in our focus groups did feel threatened by immigration, and, as we saw in Chapter 3, they also felt that tough rhetoric and highly visible government enforcement campaigns were intended to reassure them (as 'ordinary people'), that something was being done. But some also saw through this rhetoric. The populist call did not always convince them that the government was any more in tune with them. This was what was conveyed in a focus group interview in Barking and Dagenham, quoted in Chapter 2. As Alan put it: 'They're [the Home Office] trying to give the idea to the general public that they're doing something about it, but they're doing absolutely nothing.'

In James Brokenshire's speech, the Minister positions himself as on the side of 'ordinary, hard-working people' rather than callous employers or wealthy elites. There is a profound irony to this declaration made by a government minister to an audience at a London think tank – the very epitome of the 'wealthy metropolitan elite'. But of course, the 'metropolitan elite' are always elsewhere. They are figures of speech that enable concerns about immigration control (in this instance) to be positioned as out of touch with gritty reality, as a fancy of those with too much money and/or education, who live in a protected 'bubble'. The 'ordinary people' are positioned as a 'silent majority' without the economic, social or cultural capital to access forums used by the 'elite' (such as newspaper columns, broadcasters or particular forms of social media such as Twitter). This is a very similar position to how an idea of the 'white working class' is used in British political discourses of the early twentieth century (Haylett, 2001). Brokenshire can then claim to speak on behalf of a beleaguered minority, without making reference to his position and that of his immediate audience as part of a class (as politicians and establishment journalists and policy-makers) which is both elite and institutionally closed off.[2]

Fears that other people ('them') might be doing better than 'us' ('ordinary people') are not investigated, much less addressed, by interventions like Brokenshire's. Rather, fears are re-created and inflamed (see also Ahmed, 2008). In doing so, a divide between 'us' and 'them', between 'ordinary people' and others is widened. This leaves little space for recognition of points of commonality or 'ordinariness' among people whose lives are different. It closes down the opportunities to see migrants, refugees and asylum seekers as part of the an imaginary 'ordinary people' on whose behalf the Home Office

---

[2] 51 per cent of the UK's leading journalists, 32 per cent of MPs, and 74 per cent of top judges were privately educated (compared to an estimated 7 per cent of the population as a whole); 54 per cent of journalists, 47 per cent of Cabinet ministers, and 74 per cent of judges in the UK in 2016 attended the same two universities (compared to less than 1 per cent of the population as a whole) (Kirby, 2016).

Minister might have obligations of care and responsibility. At the same time, there are complexities to this seemingly stark divide in which pro-migration activism is also ensnared. For example, in the 'I am an immigrant' campaign discussed in Chapter 5, which aimed to combat xenophobia by highlighting the lives of high-achieving migrants, a full spectrum of migrant lives – such as those who are not socially successful or might even be claiming welfare benefits – is obscured. In such idealised, or perhaps normative, representations, migrants are still not allowed to be 'ordinary'. They must be extraordinary.

Racism and immigration

> Our minds are conditioned to think of our nations as maps and flags rather than collections of actual people. If only we can love humanity rather than maps, we'd all be much happier.
>
> (Shivam Vij, 2012: n.p.)

Throughout this book, we have argued that an understanding of immigration control at this contemporary moment must engage with questions of race and racism and their intersections with other social differences. Sometimes this link can be hard to grasp – surely immigration laws are about nationality, not race or ethnicity? Aren't most countries in the world multiethnic anyway, in which case isn't it actually 'racist' to say there is an association between immigration laws and race? By focusing on racialised differences aren't you actually being racist? An exemplary version of this refusal to recognise any association between racism and immigration control was the Conservative Party's 2005 election slogan, 'it's not racist to impose limits on immigration'.

Such refusals are not just straightforward denials. They engage with an affective register of affront. Sarita Srivastava (2005) has written lucidly about the way that the enraged, hurt cry 'are you calling me a racist?' shifts conversations that are begun to address institutionalised discrimination. Instead, they become focused on tending to the injured feelings of the person who has been accused of racism. The logic is that racism is recognised by all as bad; therefore accusing someone of racist behaviour is among the worst accusations. There is no space for asking how such feelings of hurt or affront compare to being the subject of racist acts or a racist system (see also Ahmed, 2010, on feminist killjoys).

Our work on this book is not a project to demonstrate racism at work in immigration control, in order to demonise those responsible and therefore leave questions neatly solved. We are more interested in how current forms of immigration control and related discussions tend to close down debate about discrimination and race, whilst those forces remain unchallenged. As we see it, the tactic of separating narratives of immigration control from discussions of racism is complicit with the sorting and enforcement processes of bordering. It produces new forms and consequences of racialisation, where the *idea* of race as an absolute difference has real effects, such as dispossession, slavery and death, what Lentin identifies as 'crimes ... that mark and shape whole groups of people, often for generations' (2008: 497). These crimes – physical and psychic – are also entangled with forces of displacement, exile and statelessness. In this way, immigration, or, rather, immigration control and bordering practices cannot be understood without a historical understanding of racism and colonialism, and of how these are entangled with more recent discourses of multiculturalism and migration. We note, with Gurminder K. Bhambra (2016), the insidiousness of European immigration discourses and policies that are based upon racialised class divides. As Sandro Mezzadra and Brett Neilson (2008: n.p.) remind us, 'borders in the contemporary global order serve not simply as devices of exclusion but as technologies of differential inclusion'.

Traces of the complicated relationships between race, racism and immigration control are visible in our research. Aside from the Go Home van, another mobile technology of demonstrating the toughness of immigration control was the introduction of a more visible liveried set of vehicles for immigration enforcement officers to use when on patrols and raids. When Ipsos MORI asked British adults who were aware of these immigration enforcement branded vans on UK streets how they felt about seeing them (see Appendix for methodological details), 31 per cent said they felt reassured that the government was taking action against illegal or irregular immigration; 28 per cent said it made them concerned that some people are being treated with unnecessary suspicion in everyday situations. And 16 per cent said it made them think that illegal or irregular immigration might be more widespread than they had realised. This suggests that, like many of the measures used to demonstrate 'toughness', these vans barely reassure more people than they worry – and they actually increase worry among a significant number of people who see them.

But then we looked at the breakdown between the reactions of white respondents, and racially minoritised respondents, to that question. More white respondents (34 per cent) were reassured that the government was taking action against irregular or illegal immigration than for the population as a whole. And far fewer 'BME' respondents (21 per cent) were reassured by these Immigration Enforcement vans.

This was reversed somewhat for those who were concerned that the vans might indicate that some people were being treated with unnecessary suspicion – only 25 per cent of white respondents thought this, but 36 per cent of 'BME' respondents. That is, racially minoritised ('BME') respondents were much more likely to see the enforcement vans as an intervention that could result in unfair treatment. They were also significantly more likely to be aware of these vans (23 per cent) than white respondents (16 per cent).

This suggests to us a connection between being able to see oneself in a situation, and how one reacts to it. That racially minoritised respondents were so much more likely than the white respondents to worry about people being treated with unfair suspicion as a result of more highly visible immigration enforcement raids may well have something to do with their experience – directly or indirectly – of being unfairly treated with suspicion in similar situations. As Lucee, a woman from Sierra Leone who had been granted refugee status and was settled in Bradford, told us during a focus group:

> And for example like where I live it's like predominantly white people and I'm not saying like white, all of them, but there have been a few racist things going on, so, and these are people who obviously don't care whether I've got my stay or not, every time they've seen me they've always told me to go back to my country. So imagine if they saw this [the Go Home van] they'd probably call them, pick me up [laughs] do you know?
>
> (Bradford Focus Group, conducted by Hannah)

Lucee had not seen the van herself and was not subject to immigration enforcement any more. Yet she feared the government campaigns because of the way she imagined them creating or further legitimising the xenophobia and racism she had experienced from her neighbours. Not only that, she also pointed to the way that suspicions (about immigration status) become attached to particular bodily markers, such as her dark brown skin and her West African accent (see also Rita's experience explored in Chapters 2 and 4).

'Relatable' migrants

In February 2015, Hannah and Kirsten were asked to speak about our research at an event organised by the Detention Forum, a charity that campaigns for the rights of people in immigration detention in the UK (see also Living Research Three). At the main offices of Amnesty International in East London, they sat on a panel along with Harley Miller, an Australian whose dispute with the Home Office over her leave to remain in the UK had become a public campaign issue. Other panellists were Ian Dunt, an online journalist who has written on migration issues; and Aderonke Apata, a Nigerian lesbian facing deportation after a High Court judge ruled that she had 'fabricated' her sexuality in order to settle in Britain (Dugan, 2014). At this meeting, we were struck by comments from Ian Dunt to the effect that news and comment stories about migration (or anything else) needed to be 'relatable', that is, in order to care about an issue, or even read to the end of an article, readers should be able to see that it could happen to them or someone close to them. In other words, they had to see the protagonists as 'ordinary people'. To this end, he argued that stories such as Harley's (or cases of non-EU spouses separated from their UK partners by immigration law) were more meaningful to most people in the UK, and therefore more likely to be picked up by news outlets and politicians, than experiences like Aderonke's or those of others held in immigration detention.

The fact that such language and assumptions are mundane does not make them less powerful or, indeed, violent in their consequences. In fact, we might argue that it is in the very banality of such assumptions that their power lies. The shock that broke through when the British government associated itself publicly with the racists' slogan 'go home' mobilised political action and outrage. But when the less spectacular identification of some British residents as undeserving of care or innately suspicious (for example, through reminders in NHS waiting rooms that 'hospital treatment is not free for everyone' (see Chapter 2), or alerts to enforcement actions in the local press) becomes unremarkable, the process of excluding (some) migrants from what Bridget Anderson terms the 'community of value' (2013) is much more powerful.

Similar dynamics have been described by the psychosocial theorist Gail Lewis (2007), invoking and developing Raymond Williams's (1958) work on ordinary culture to show that 'racialising culture is ordinary' too:

> such cultural practices stand right at the heart of contemporary everyday life and mediate individual experiences and the social relations of 'race', gender, class, sexuality, and age. Moreover ... hegemonic projects are never fully achieved, are always unstable, making possible forms of appropriation, destabilization and change. Thus, whilst cultural practices of racialization occur within networks of power and contestation their trajectories and outcomes are never certain, never guaranteed.
>
> (Lewis, 2007: 873)

This second point in Lewis's quote is important. We have tried, throughout the book, to understand the rippling effects of government communications on immigration control – and to recognise the contradictions and unexpected consequences as well as those that might have been predictable to some. The racialising logics of a claim that solidarity with 'ordinary people' can only come from association with 'people like us' – where the 'us' is in the imagination of the (white, male) London journalist and therefore vested in citizens of majority-white countries whose heteronormative families or respectable career paths are interrupted by immigration control – seems clear to us (the authors), given our training as social scientists. They are not obvious to all, and they are worth unpicking and analysing for the record, as a part of public debate, which too often goes unacknowledged.

However, we do not want to stop our analysis there, at the point of 'racism is everywhere', because we have seen more than that. Lewis, and others, remind us that the process of racialisation, like other social struggles over power, is never finished, it evolves and changes and is therefore unpredictable. The identification of some people on the sharp end of immigration control who are 'ordinary people' opens up the question of who an ordinary person might be, and in what manner they are ordinary. Similarly, the re-entry of immigration into public debate in the UK over the last twenty years has unsettled a seeming settlement about the place of 'ethnic minorities' in British society. The reminders of colonial processes, which led former British colonial subjects to the UK, are roused again by the arrival of new movements of populations from other parts of the globe. New kinds of resistance, identification and rejection form in response to this, as we have seen throughout the book and especially in Chapters 4 and 5. So when we agree that racialising culture is ordinary, and that we might see many instances of immigration control in the present moment as part of a process of racialisation, that does not mean that old logics of racism and opposition are being produced in the same formations as in the past.

As we heard in Chapter 4 from Rita, opposition to new migration is not restricted to white British-born residents, as she witnessed opposition to immigration from local Asian people in Southall and was 'shocked, my Asian community they hate us … My Asian community hate Asian people, it was so sad.' Similarly, Mark, a pro-migrant activist in London, told Sukhwant that 'one of the scariest things we're seeing … at the moment is migrant communities thinking it's a good idea to stop immigration'. As we discussed in Chapter 5, there are multiple forces at work here in reconfiguring who is seen (by whom) as part of a 'community of value' worthy of being part of the nation. Not only that, but those who are at the edges of a community of value sometimes have more at stake in distinguishing themselves from the 'real' outsiders by participating in these processes of what we would call racialisation, though it may not be along the lines predicted by received ideas about racial divisions.

The appeal to toughness in the government campaigns we have been following attempts to seal off – or at least bypass – this complexity, to produce a postpolitical consensus (as discussed in Chapter 2). As we saw in Chapter 3, these campaigns seem to create a self-perpetuating problem – can government measures ever be thorough enough to get migration 'under control'? In a world that is ever more mobile, and where capitalism relies on the movement of people – not just as labour but where the immigration-industrial complex is increasingly an arena for private profit (see Anderson, 2014) – migration control seems to be reduced to a performance, albeit a performance with real and dire consequences. While migration is seen as a threat in need of control, and that control has to be visibly performed, how can anyone be safe from either migration or migration control, except, as we saw in Chapter 5, by positioning themselves as less of a threat than some 'other' group?

Stuart Hall coined the term 'multicultural drift' to recognise 'the increasing visible presence of black and Asian people in all aspects of British social life', not as 'the result of deliberate and planned policy', but rather 'the unintended outcome of undirected sociological processes' (1999: 188). We might say that a similar process is now under way, not simply of migration becoming or having become an everyday aspect of life but (perhaps more of a departure) migration *control* and anti-migrant rhetoric have become mundane. The drift of migration enforcement into the banal tasks of education administrators (see Back, 2016: 32–6), human resources departments, private landlords and healthcare professionals is accompanied by a drift of migration talk, migration suspicion and endless debate about who has the right to resources and to existence in a specific national space. In what ways might the research presented in this book help us not only to understand, but also to intervene in those conversations?

Conversations

We must create a polyphony, a tune of many voices that is truth for all of us.

(Syed Khalid Hussan, 2013: 281)

Not everyone thinks that being ordinary means being identical to themselves, or that either of those things equates to a person being worthy of care and basic quality of life. When politicians and others appeal on behalf of ordinary people, this is not a call of solidarity. Instead, they are reasserting the political voicelessness of those groups, rather than listening to their concerns. In a classic work of cultural studies, *Policing the Crisis,* Stuart Hall and colleagues described such moves when made by news media as 'taking the public voice' (1978: 63). What we have tried to do in this book and this project is to recognise a multiplicity of ordinary voices, their varying experiences and how the public performance of immigration control resonates in daily lives. We have tried not to 'take' those voices but to consider their various viewpoints and concerns seriously. In doing so, we have seen some of the ordinary effects of reproducing ideas of threat and control around immigration; a variety of unsettling senses of fear and insecurity, tempered sometimes – when anger escapes through a crack in the fear – into political solidarities and action.

We are still stuck with this dismissal of concerns about the harshness of immigration control as a preoccupation of a 'liberal metropolitan elite'. Who are they? Probably the authors of this book would be prime candidates to be included. We are all academics with decent pay who live in cities and get paid to write about the state of the world, and who care deeply about the consequences of immigration control (among other things). But we are also ordinary people. We all have families, friends and homes that we care about, both spread across the UK and overseas. Most of us have some form of migration history in our lives or the lives of our families; some more immediate than others. We are affected when public services are underfunded, and when housing becomes unaffordable – though we are able to cope with this, at this point in our lives, in ways that people with less economic means might not be. We recognise this. And we don't think our privilege or our pain means that those who do not share them are less 'ordinary' than us, or less worthy of a decent life.

We also know that thousands of other people, ordinary and extraordinary, do share our concerns; we know this because they have told us so through our research, because we have seen them mobilising in political demonstrations, because we have seen them give of their time, energy and resources to help others. This is not an elite but a hotchpotch of people with different motivations and experiences, different kinds of privilege and vulnerability, and different views, but enough in common to be concerned about what the consequences of immigration control outlined in this book are doing not just to individuals at the sharp end but to our democracy and common humanity.

These concerns don't always get articulated in the same ways. The performance politics of immigration control set out not only to demonstrate toughness and control held by government, they mask or dismiss the everyday pain and uncertainty of varying intensities that immigration *control* causes, that touch increasingly on everyone's lives. This might range from the (ordinary) person renting out a property, who must take responsibility for their tenants' residency papers being in order, under threat of possible imprisonment; to the (ordinary) person seeking a home to rent but whom landlords avoid as soon as they hear that person's 'foreign-sounding' name (Grant and Peel, 2015); to the (ordinary) person whose children are in danger in a home country but is refused refugee status, and then sees no prospect of them being safe other than undertaking a treacherous journey by land and sea with the hope of a new home, but the risk of death. These stories are not headline news. But when we think of Ian Dunt's seemingly common-sense explanation about what makes something newsworthy, we might also think back to Hall et al.'s (1978) demonstration of how that which becomes news is also that which serves a dominant narrative, or hegemony.

As we discussed in Living Research Five, a key motivator in our research was anger; anger about social injustice, anger at repugnantly racist and xenophobic immigration control narratives and practices becoming normalised. We channelled this anger through our professional training as social researchers to find out more about the dynamics and consequences of what had angered us. And throughout the process (as described in Living Research Six), we have tried to do this in conversation and collaboration with people more embedded in these currents, from activists to policy-makers to refugees to those feeling threatened by immigration. This process has been a conversation, and as a conversation our intention has always been to continue the exchange, to proffer our analysis, findings and theorisations to add to and perhaps enrich in a small way the public conversation.

One way in which we have done this is simply through the focus of our research. As we noted in Chapter 2, we aimed to focus less on attitudes to 'immigration', towards an understanding of how government campaigns about immigration worked, and their consequences for different audiences. Another attempted shift is in our aim to treat our research as what Les Back (2007) describes as a 'listener's art', bringing conflicting and neglected perspectives together, not simply to 'give voice' but through our attention and analysis giving weight to those voices; unpeeling some of the layers of contradiction, conflict and surprising affinities in understandings of migration (and its control), which can too often be easily polarised.

Our research has deliberately been intended as public scholarship, work using rigorous academic methods while engaging with collaborators and audiences beyond the university. In recent years there has been much discussion of public sociology attached to an address by Professor Michael Burawoy (2005) to the American Sociological Association. We have looked more widely and further back to root our ethos of public scholarship with thinkers such as W.E.B. Du Bois, bell hooks, Audre Lorde and Angela Davis, whose scholarly writing was a part of their activism, always to inform social struggles and make ideas accessible to publics beyond universities.

But of course, the conversation shifts regardless of scholarly intervention, and often unpredictably in relation to world events, policy changes, or chance incidents, which break through the cracks of what seems a settled conclusion. In a blog post in September 2015, in the days after Alan Kurdi's death became a global spectacle (see Chapter 1), Hannah wrote:

> The tone of the public reaction is shifting fast. We're starting to hear less about the threat posed by these people and more about the 'unbearable' sight of a three-year-old boy washed up, dead, on the shore of Turkey, and everything it implies.
>
> (Jones, 2015)

At that moment, the shocking image of Alan's body breached the apparent certainties about border control, and brought 'ordinary people' across Europe on to the streets in support of welcoming more refugees into their homes. In a sense nothing had changed with the death of Alan; children had been dying on that same crossing and others for months and years. But until then, none had been captured in an image that so eloquently broke through the xenophobic rhetoric and performative politics of the UK government and others. As we have noted in Chapter 1, a shift did occur in public debate – but it was short-lived. In the UK, the then Prime Minister Cameron's promise that Britain would take twenty thousand Syrian refugees from UN camps over five years seemed to close down the debate, allowing some to feel that a problem had been addressed. This despite the criticisms that this gesture amounted to a relatively small number of refugees compared to either the national population or the number of refugees worldwide; that adequate resources to support those even that would be given refuge had not been made available to local government; that by only taking people through the UN resettlement scheme nothing was done to address the plight of people already in Europe seeking sanctuary; and that by restricting the scheme to Syrians, victims of other conflicts less covered by European media continued to be ignored.

In trying to engage in public scholarship we will sometimes be outrun by changing developments. As we try to highlight shifts in circumstances and their significance, they just as quickly change again. In our research and this book we have tried to avoid such an ephemeral engagement. We have noted how a set of individually short-lived interventions – the Go Home van, visibility of enforcement raids, reminders of immigration control in everyday life – together present a more significant trend: the drift of immigration enforcement, of an obsession with borders and of hatred, into the ongoing concerns of ordinary life.

We should not forget that what is at stake is not simply a conversation, but has material, harsh consequences. This includes the death, detention and destitution faced by Aderonke Apata and Alan Kurdi; the unheard lives of others in indefinite immigration detention, living in destitution, in fear of deportation, separated from families; and those like Joe, Carol and Alan whom we heard in Chapter 2, scared by immigration and its effects in their local areas, fearing new migrants as an uncontrollable threat to jobs, homes and prosperity. We should note too, that the material consequences of the drift towards the everyday mobilisation of the border and immigration control can sometimes be generative – bringing people together in new ways to mobilise politically, perhaps because the connections between different types of 'ordinary people' affected by immigration control become clearer, or as people who previously thought immigration control relevant only to 'other people' start to respond to this very everyday reality.

We hope that the many interactions that have been a part of this book will continue, as people read and talk about what we have written here. These are small attempts to make a shift, with others, in how we think about immigration control in our everyday lives. Ultimately it is a plea to recognise our common humanity.

And it is an unfinished, unfolding conversation.

Postscript

In the final days of preparing our manuscript for publication, we were reading back through what we had written, thinking carefully about the claims we have been making about the relationships between the performative politics of immigration policing campaigns and increasing xenophobia, intolerance and racism. It was during this time that the Labour MP Jo Cox, an active advocate for the rights of migrants and those seeking asylum, was violently murdered on 16 June 2016 (see also Chapter 1). During his court appearance, the murder suspect Thomas Mair was asked to confirm his name and replied: 'My name is death to traitors, freedom for Britain'. Like thousands of others, from all walks of life and from all parts of the globe, we were horrified and angered at this murder. The thought that it had been motivated by a hatred for a young woman whose compassion for others was felt to be so deeply treacherous and threatening was sickening. 'Jo's killing was political, it was an act of terror designed to advance an agenda of hatred towards others', said Cox's husband in a moving speech given at Trafalgar Square to celebrate what would have been Jo Cox's forty-second birthday on 22 June (Addley et al., 2016). Brendan Cox went on:

> What a beautiful irony it is that an act designed to advance hatred has instead generated such an outpouring of love. Jo lived for her beliefs, and on Thursday she died for them, and for the rest of our lives we will fight for them in her name.

As we complete this project in the wake of the June 2016 EU referendum result, reports have been appearing in the mainstream press and social media of an increase in xenophobic and racist abuse and violence. We do not know yet exactly how widespread this is or whether the narrative of 'taking control' of our borders and immigration that was so prominent in the Leave campaign will continue, or kindle new forms of nationalism and racism (see Davies, 2016).

It need not be this way. We hope that the conversations into which we have invited you might contribute to the collective work of imagining and building a more inclusive future for us all.

References

Addley, E., Elgot, J. and Perraudin, F. (2016) 'Jo Cox: Thousands pay tribute on what should have been MP's birthday', www.theguardian.com/uk-news/2016/jun/22/jo-cox-murder-inspired-more-love-than-hatred-says-husband-brendan [last accessed 25 June 2016].

Ahmed, S. (2008) ' "Liberal multiculturalism is the hegemony – it's an empirical fact" – a response to Slavoj Žižek', *Dark Matter*,

19 February, www.darkmatter101.org/site/2008/02/19/ per centE2 per cent80 per cent98liberal-multiculturalism-is-the-hegemony-per centE2 per cent80 per cent93-its-an-empirical-fact per centE2 per cent80 per cent99-a-response-to-slavoj-zizek/.

Ahmed, S. (2010) 'Feminist killjoys (and other willful subjects)', *The Scholar and Feminist Online*, 8 (3), http://sfonline.barnard.edu/polyphonic/ahmed_01.htm#text1 [last accessed 22 May 2016].

Anderson, B. (2013) *Us and Them? The Dangerous Politics of Immigration Control*, Oxford: Oxford University Press.

Anderson, R. (2014) *Illegality, Inc: Clandestine Migration and the Business of Bordering Europe*, Oakland: University of California Press.

Asthana, A., Quinn, B. and Mason, M. (2016) 'Britain votes to leave EU after dramatic night divides nation', www.theguardian.com/politics/2016/jun/24/britain-votes-for-brexit-eu-referendum-david-cameron [last accessed 25 June 2016].

Back, L. (2007) *The Art of Listening*, London: Berg.

Back, L. (2016) *Academic Diary: Or Why Higher Education Still Matters*, London: Goldsmiths Press.

Back, L., Keith, M., Khan, A., Shukra, K. and Solomos, J. (2002) 'New Labour's white heart: politics, multiculturalism and the return of assimilation', *The Political Quarterly*, 73 (4): 445–54.

Bhambra, G. (2016) 'Whither Europe? Postcolonial versus neocolonial cosmopolitanism', *Interventions: International Journal of Postcolonial Studies*, 17(2): 187–202.

Blair, T. (2000) *Speech at the World Economic Forum at Davos, Switzerland*, 18 January, http://webarchive.nationalarchives.gov.uk/20060715135117/number10.gov.uk/page1508 [last accessed 22 May 2016].

Blinder, S. (2015) *Briefing: Migration to the UK: Asylum*, 4th revision, Oxford: The Migration Observatory, http://www.migrationobservatory.ox.ac.uk/sites/files/migobs/Briefing per cent20-per cent20Migration per cent20to per cent20the per cent20UK per cent20- per cent20Asylum_0.pdf [last accessed 22 May 2016].

Brokenshire, J. (2014) *James Brokenshire MP, Minister for Immigration and Security, Ppeech to the Think Tank Demos*, 6 March, London: Demos, www.demos.co.uk/files/JamesBrokenshireSpeechtoDemos.pdf [last accessed 22 May 2016].

Burawoy, M. (2005) 'For public sociology', *American Sociological Review*, 70: 4–28.

Cabinet Office (2001) *Migration: An Economic and Social Analysis*, London: Her Majesty's Stationery Office.

Davies, W. (2016) 'Thoughts on the sociology of Brexit, 24 June 2016', www.perc.org.uk/project_posts/thoughts-on-the-sociology-of-brexit/ [last accessed 25 June 2016].

Dugan, E. (2014) 'Aderonke Apata deportation case: "If the Home Office doesn't believe I'm gay, I'll send them a video that proves it"', *The Independent*, 8 June, www.independent.co.uk/news/uk/home-news/aderonke-apata-deportation-case-if-the-home-office-doesnt-believe-i-m-gay-i-ll-send-them-a-video-9509738.html [last accessed 22 May 2016].

Grant, S. and Peel, C. (2015) *'No Passport Equals No Home':An Independent Evaluation of the 'Right to Rent' Scheme*, London: JCWI.

Hall, S. (1999) 'From Scarman to Stephen Lawrence', *History Workshop Journal*, 48: 187–97.

Hall, S., Crichter, C., Jefferson, T., Clarke, J. and Roberts, B. (1978) *Policing the Crisis: Mugging, the State and Law and Order*, London: Macmillan.

Haylett, C. (2001) 'Illegitimate subjects?: Abject whites, neoliberal modernisation, and middle-class multiculturalism', *Environment and Planning D: Society and Space*, 19 (3): 351–70.

Home Office (2002) *Secure Borders, Safe Heaven: Integration with Diversity in Modern Britain*, London: The Stationery Office.

Hussan, S.K. (2013) 'Epilogue', in H. Walia, *Undoing Border Imperialism*, Edinburgh: AK Press/Institute of Anarchist Studies, pp. 277–84.

Jones, H. (2015) 'Public opinion on the refugee crisis is changing fast – and for the better', *The Conversation*, 4 September, http://theconversation.com/public-opinion-on-the-refugee-crisis-is-changing-fast-and-for-the-better-47064 [last accessed 22 May 2016].

Kirby, P. (2016) *Leading People 2016: The Educational Backgrounds of the UK Professional Elite*, London: The Sutton Trust.

Lentin, A. (2008) 'Europe and the silence about race', *European Journal of Social Theory*, 11 (4): 487–503.

Lewis, G. (2007) 'Racializing culture is ordinary', *Cultural Studies*, 21 (6): 866–86.

Machin, S. (2015) 'Real wages and living standards: The latest UK evidence', *LSE British Politics and Policy Blog*, http://blogs.lse.ac.uk/politicsandpolicy/real-wages-and-living-standards/ [last accessed 23 May 2016].

Mezzadra, S. and Neilson, B. (2008) 'Border as method, or, the multiplication of labor', *EIPCP*, http://eipcp.net/transversal/0608/mezzadraneilson/en [last accessed 19 September 2016].

Srivastava, S. (2005) ' "You're calling me a racist?" The moral and emotional regulation of antiracism and feminism', *Signs*, 31 (1): 29–62.

Stonor Saunders, F. (2016) 'Where on earth are you?', *London Review of Books*, 3 March, 38 (5): 7–12.

Vargas-Silva, C. and Markaki, Y. (2015) *Briefing: EU Migration to and from UK*, Oxford: Migration Observatory.

Vij, S. (2012) 'Of nationalism and love in Southasia', *Himal SouthAsian*, 19 June 2012, http://himalmag.com/of-nationalism-and-love-in-southasia/ [last accessed 8 July 2016].

Williams, R. (1958) 'Culture is ordinary', in N. Mackenzie (ed.), *Conviction*, London: MacGibbon and Kee, pp. 74–92.

Williams, R. (1983/1976) *Keywords: A Vocabulary of Culture and Society*, revised edition. Oxford: Oxford University Press.

Living Research Six: Collaborations

Our research on Operation Vaken was rooted in several different forms of engagement, with the hope not only of intervening in social injustices (see Passy, 2001) but also of producing knowledge differently; a less elitist and collaborative knowledge. The root of the word collaboration, from the Latin *collaborare* – to work together – carries ambivalence. To collaborate can also suggest betrayal, even treachery. Here we discuss what was involved in our research relationships, from those between ourselves as academic activists and 'resisting others' (Autonomous Geographies Collective, 2010: 248) to our work with an established, profit-making research company, which we subsequently found also carried out work for the Home Office.

We will try to describe as best we can what we did to deal with conflicting pressures and approaches in our partnerships, highlighting what we learnt. As the feminist theorist Robyn Wiegman (2012) has argued so brilliantly, our attachments to radical alternative futures can often come at a price, including a seductive delusion in how we read and diagnose the *status quo* and possibilities for transformation. There can be a tendency to close down ambivalence, Weigman believes, in order to tell a particular version of a story – one in which we know best.

Building collaborations

Researcher-activists working across a range of social-justice platforms spend a huge amount of time thinking, talking and theorising about – and researching – how to make meaningful interventions. Researchers do not hold all the interpretative cards, but they may add something in terms of intellectual resources, skills and methodologies. In our case, our research funding was also able to support and recognise the research work of our partner organisations.

One of the most fundamental partnerships in our project was how we worked with each other. Noting the largely individualised accounts of activist researchers (Autonomous Geographies Collective, 2010), we believe that the very fact we came together as a group is important. As a large research team, we corresponded regularly in group email exchanges and scheduled intensive meetings over the course of the research to plan and to discuss troubles, successes and new ideas. We were able to write together, as well as to contribute and comment on each other's blog posts, draft papers and conference presentations. When our ways of working were sometimes questioned within some university regimes, we were able to defend and support ourselves by making reference to our commitments to the wider research team.

Our team comprised some people whose experience of activism was street-level and community-facing, while others were more academically based. Some team members already worked within the frameworks of the live (Back and Puwar, 2013), inventive (Lury and Wakeford, 2012) and real-time (Gunaratnam and Back, 2015) style of sociological research that underpinned the study; others were new to such approaches. The team included academics at all stages of their academic careers. As a group, we provided a critical mass of expertise that was important to the funding body and at the same time provided a support structure that allowed us to work together collectively, while operating individually with a variety of frames of reference, environmental contexts and employment statuses. Our sociological standpoints differed, yet we managed to collaborate and thrive as a large research group with a shared commitment to critical social research. Common leanings towards activist and anti-racist feminist research informed our approach and ethos and oiled the conversations, decisions and steps taken throughout the research process.

Collaboration also underpinned our work with our community research partners, many of whom we had worked with before there was any prospect of securing research funding. They helped to shape the questions we might ask and how we might ask them. It was important to us, and to the success (and ethics) of the project, that the work done by community groups to develop and support our research was properly remunerated – both because of their precarious funding and to formally value the time and expertise they provided. Our existing connections and working relationships allowed us to develop these connections relatively quickly, to exchange vital information about the project, and to engage locally.

Collaborating across sectors – in this case, between community-based organisations and large universities – is not without its challenges (Saltus, 2006). It is evident that such work requires constant negotiation and sensitivity to the different demands made upon partners, to different standpoints and sometimes to different agendas. In our working relationships, we were very much aware of the challenges faced by our community partners. These included precarious funding, staffing and time constraints and the need to prioritise face-to-face immigration work (e.g. dealing with destitution and deportation) and campaigning. Although a partnership template devised by the team was drafted, the programmes of work in our local case studies varied depending on the circumstances facing partners in each of the six areas and on the individuals who carried out the research. In some cases, we worked with more than one local organisation to ensure we captured a range of views and experiences. The degree of involvement differed, with some community research partners playing a significant role in key stages of the data-collection process (for example, facilitating focus-group discussions, and maintaining clear and steady lines of communication and engagement), with the commitments of other partners resulting in less involvement.

Our partners' approach to the research funding and their experience of this type of collaboration also varied. One organisation insisted that it could do more with the money allocated to organising two focus groups, while others took great care in facilitating access to local immigration activists and in planning for the interviews. We also had experience of the research being done more haphazardly or 'on the trot', because of staff shortages and the huge workload of a research partner. We felt unable to comment directly, knowing all the time that the organisation's services were in a precarious position and the research funding was vital. In effect, the empirical research bore the brunt of the challenges, uncertainty and instability faced by some of our partners.

On commissioning critical survey research: the questions we ask

The findings from the small-scale street survey conducted days after the launch of Operation Vaken and the Go Home vans suggested that attitudes to migration might not be so simply divided into 'for' or 'against', but were more complicated (with answers often having a 'Yes, but ...' element). We wanted to produce survey data that could reflect some of the complexity and ambivalence of public opinion on migration and its control. Linked to this, our qualitative research had revealed the understanding that 'being seen' to be tough on immigration is about performance – captured in actions, gestures, costumes (uniforms), props (enforcement vehicles) and displays (for instance the documenting and publicising of immigration raids) (see Chapter 2). All performances use triggers that work to elicit an emotional response, and so we wanted our survey to test the kinds of responses such performances might elicit. Our focus was to identify public attitudes to immigration control when faced with the realities of the techniques used as part of that control.

A common practice in UK academic research aiming for large-scale polling data is to commission this work from external companies that have the infrastructure to produce such data quickly. This is a practice we followed, engaging a large market-research company to undertake this element of the project. In negotiating the design of our survey questions – which were going to be inserted into the company's longer weekly 'omnibus' survey – the challenges of working across different epistemological approaches and across research cultures with very different priorities (academic versus commercial) became apparent. Many of the questions we originally developed, and the ways we wanted to ask them, appeared 'risky' and 'emotive' to the polling company.

Negotiations over the wording (which had been carefully discussed and crafted by the team and was rooted in the original survey work done during the Go Home campaign) often focused on reframing the language to be objective and neutral. This process derived from a need to arrive at a set of 'unbiased' questions, placed within the context of established wisdom and expertise in market research (see Living Research Four for a critique of this approach). For us, an underlying tension concerned differences in how we understood the limits and the basis of polling research. A problem for us was the largely unchallenged perception that the official framing of immigration questions routinely used in such surveys is not emotive (a separate but related matter being whether any survey questions can be without emotion). Another tension was the careful development of the draft survey questions and the collaborative, iterative effort underpinning them, which remained important as a methodological and analytic framework.

One question where there seemed to be a particular mismatch between our epistemology and that of the market-research company was our attempt to get a sense of public opinion on racial profiling in immigration checks. The question of whether such profiling had been carried out was raised by Baroness Doreen Lawrence (see Chapter 1) and we wanted to find evidence of whether the general population thought such practices were acceptable. During the process of negotiating the commissioned research, this question went through several iterations. Our original version was as follows:

> Eyewitnesses have suggested that white people are less likely to be questioned during immigration raids and checks. Do you think it is acceptable to target people for immigration checks on the basis of their appearance? [You can choose more than one option]
> a   Yes, it saves time and resources
> b   Yes, if you have done nothing wrong you have nothing to fear
> c   No, it can lead to persecution of British people
> d   No, it is racist
> e   Something else [record open-ended answer]
>> (Original question in commissioning request
>> by Mapping Immigration Controversy (MIC) team
>> to Ipsos MORI, July 2014)

This question became something quite different in one draft we were sent:

> ASK ALL
> WU07. In your opinion do you think the Home Office Immigration Enforcement team target particular types of people during immigration raids, or not?
> (DP: SINGLE CODE, RAN)
> Yes
> No
> Don't know
> IF WU07 = CODES 1, THEN ASK WU08
> WU08. You said you thought the Home Office Immigration Enforcement team target particular types of people during immigration raids. What type of people do you think they target and why?
> Please type in as many reasons as apply
> (DP: ALLOW DK)
> (OPEN ENDED)
>> (Revised question in email from Ipsos MORI to Hannah,
>> 13 August 2014)

On receiving this draft, Hannah asked for 'a discussion of why this has been changed so radically, especially since I have explained our objective with this question was to ask whether people thought racial profiling in immigration checks was acceptable/appropriate, not to ask the general population to guess at whether or not this goes on' (Hannah's email to MIC team, 13 August 2014). In the end, a question closer to what we wished to ask was restored to the corpus:

ASK ALL
WU07. Some people have suggested that white people are less likely to be questioned during checks or raids on suspected irregular/illegal immigrants. How acceptable or unacceptable, do you think it would be if immigration officers carried out checks on the basis of someone's skin colour?
(DP: SINGLE CODE, FORWARD AND REVERSE LIST)
1   Very acceptable
2   Fairly acceptable
3   No opinion either way
4   Fairly unacceptable
5   Very unacceptable
6   Don't know
IF WU07 = CODES 1–5, THEN ASK WU08A
WU08A. Why do you say that?
(DP: ALLOW DK)
(OPEN ENDED)
> (Question used on Ipsos MORI Capibus survey for MIC
> project, between 15 August and 9 September 2014)

For us, the prompts (drawn from our preliminary street-survey work and qualitative data) were key in shifting the register in which immigration is so often framed in national polls. They did this in ways that allowed an exploration of concerns about the racist and violent impacts of everyday immigration control. This is an extremely challenging ambition when dealing not only with quite different starting points about 'neutrality' and the production of knowledge, but also with the commercial and political imperatives of potential survey partners.

Additionally, in the context of commissioning commercial survey companies to conduct research as an element of a larger academic study, matters of ownership and dissemination become important. Most companies place a high premium on their rights to, and ownership of, the data collected – and, moreover, wish to control how the findings are disseminated. Although to some extent understandable in terms of wanting to ensure the integrity and reputation of their business – and to be able to build on the findings of previous polls in similar areas – the contractual terms and conditions in place risk subsuming the intellectual labour of the commissioning body, in this case the research team. Of equal importance, such contractual framings can work to sever the ties that may connect the survey activity with linked work programmes that stand outside the commissioned work. In our case, these were the qualitative elements of the project from which many of the survey questions emerged, and our ability to publish from that integrated work without interference.

Collaborative knowledge-sharing and representation

Towards the end of the project, we organised a national conference and a series of smaller, targeted events to share emerging analysis and what we had learnt. The aim was to create platforms in which to showcase the findings from the study and to offer collaborative spaces for the range of stakeholders to come together to explore immigration debates, campaigns and performative politics (see Chapter 2). As Ravensbergen and VanderPlaat (2010) have argued, although text remains a dominant part of the production, analysis and dissemination of research findings, this can involve exclusions, not least in matters of representation. For the end-of-project event, we set ourselves a task of finding ways to include people most affected by the anti-immigration campaigns. The conference placed 'beyond-text' methods (Spencer, 2011; Beebeejaum et al., 2014) – such as film- and performance-based provocations – alongside text-laden presentations, and it privileged participant dialogue over 'talking heads'. For us, the conference was as much about creating spaces for engagement and creative exploration as it was about problema-tising established forms of dissemination that can silence voices and knowledge outside the confines of academia.

A group of storytellers from the Hope Projects was one of the performance-based provocations at the conference. Founded in 2003 in the Midlands, the Hope Projects is a user-led organisation that works to empower destitute asylum-seekers and others barred from public funds. The organisation runs a number of activities, including a group for storytelling. The group performs around the UK, drawing on its own stories of forced exile, arrival and settlement journeys, as well as composite stories taken from the many other people they have met or have been told about who share a similar experience of forced migration. At the conference, the group gave a performance, with each member telling a story; they then all shared their views and reflections in a short question-and-answer session.[1]

Hannah asked the first question, enquiring how the group felt about performing their stories to an audience. The question, which pointed to something that had troubled us for a while, raises a number of issues in terms of critical research and its focus on collaboration, intervention and transformation. Of importance are the politics of storytelling – not least, storytelling by those whose personal narratives have been shaped by the move from what is understood as a personal trauma to an asylum application set within the context of political aggression and legal discourse (Shuman and Bohmer, 2004, cited in Pulitano, 2013: 117). In subsequent retellings (in everyday life), migrants must often respond to questions about their arrival and settlement.

However, the members of the Hope Projects responded to Hannah's question by explaining that for them the act of storytelling in this context was cathartic. Giving expression to painful stories can be an important part of a healing process, as the first performer stated when she stood to talk:

> We are not actors; we are just a group of women from the Hope Projects. We will try and tell you our story ... I don't like to talk about my story because always when I start, I cry. But I will try today.
>
> (Member of the Hope Projects, MIC End-of-Project Conference, June 2015)

Other performers said that narrating their own – and other people's – experiences was one way to ensure that they themselves became and remained visible; that their stories were told and heard. From the performance, we gained insights into how some people taking this particular journey have sought to understand and give meaning to their lives and their shifting social worlds. The group suggested that our conference and spaces like it provided a space to share what they wanted to share, and to tell their stories the way they wanted to tell them.

---

[1] You can watch the whole performance, and listen to the questions and answers here: www.youtube.com/watch?v=RRqUAF5G1mY [last accessed 1 July 2016].

The research feedback sessions we held in each of the local research sites went some way to circulating stories that had been shared with us by research participants. Each session provided an opportunity for the researchers and community partners to communicate both local and overall emerging findings, so participants could hear our analysis of their own situations both separately and within the context of the wider project. Questions were asked, comments raised and further points made, and we used these interactions to inform our ongoing thinking and analysis. In some cases, participants added further context. In others, they seemed satisfied to have heard the outcomes of the research in which they had participated. These were some of the ways we sought to mediate the sharing of stories and experiences within the formal research-gathering context. Those who attended the end-of-project events were there to hear about the findings, and were given an opportunity to reflect on their views, experiences and knowledge, and to share these with others.

Of equal importance to us was finding ways to extend the research findings to different audiences. One way we did this was through a short film about the research, commissioned and produced for us in the last six months of the project by the feminist film-maker Samantha Asumadu.[2] Since it became available, the film has been used in university teaching and by activist groups, as well as circulating online. It can be considered an example of an output that has travelled beyond academic circles (see also Chapter 1).

We also disseminated findings through policy briefings in Westminster and Glasgow, to showcase the study's findings to government and policy-makers in particular, and to the wider immigration and asylum-rights communities in general. The London event, a breakfast policy briefing, comprised short presentations by the research team; reflections from Pragna Patel of Southall Black Sisters (one of the community research partners); questions and comments from the audience; and a showing of our film. In a space not necessarily conducive to dialogic creativity, the use of film to convey different facets of the experience of immigration control worked well. In all three contexts – the end-of-conference event, the focus groups and feedback sessions, and the policy briefings – we tested methods of creating new types of dialogic space, but not always without constraints or compromises.

---

[2]You can view the film here: www.mappingimmigrationcontroversy.com/film.

As we have shown, there are two factors that are crucial to us in our research: close engagement and sustained collaboration with those outside of the university; and an ongoing attempt to forge more equitable methods of knowledge production. In reality, not all of our collaborations were productive. There were also many times when we did not know how things would turn out. Sometimes we were pressured – perhaps even co-opted – into uneasy and pragmatic choices. And there were many things we wish we could have done differently. This is indeed the ambivalence that comes with trying to build alternative futures and knowledge.

How would you describe collaboration? Why is collaboration important in social-justice research? How can it 'go wrong'?

What role do you think 'beyond-text' methods (e.g., performances and visual art) can play in understanding social injustice and/or in communicating social science?

What are the challenges and opportunities of critical survey design? What steps could be taken to address some of the challenges outlined above? What would you do differently?

Whose 'voice' is heard in the dissemination of research findings? What must be considered when producing multi-voiced research? What are some of the power dynamics at play?

References

Autonomous Geographies Collective (2010) 'Beyond scholar activism: Making strategic interventions inside and outside the neoliberal university', *ACME: An International E-Journal for Critical Geographers*, 9 (2): 245–75.

Back, L. and Puwar, N. (2013) *Live Methods*, Malden: Wiley-Blackwell.

Beebeejaum, Y., Durose, C., Rees, J., Richardson, J. and Richardson, L. (2014) ' "Beyond text": exploring ethos and method in co-producing research with communities', *Community Development Journal*, 49 (1): 37–53.

Gunaratnam, Y. and Back, L. (2015) 'Every minute of every day: mobilities, multiculture and time', in G Robson (ed.), *Digital Difference: Social Media and Intercultural Experience*, Newcastle: Cambridge Scholars Publishing.

Lury, C. and Wakeford, N. (2012) *Inventive Methods: The Happening of the Social*. Abingdon: Routledge.

Passy, F. (2001) 'Political altruism and the solidarity movement', in M. Guigni and F. Passy (eds), *Political Altruism? Solidarity Movements in International Perspective*, Lanham, MD: Rowman and Littlefield, pp. 3–25.

Pulitano, P. (2013) 'In liberty's shadow: the discourse of refugees and asylum seekers in critical race theory and immigration law/politics', *Identities*, 20 (2): 172–89.

Ravensbergen, F. and VanderPlaat, M. (2010) 'Barriers to citizen participation: The missing voices of people living with low income', *Community Development Review*, 45 (4): 389–403.

Saltus R. (2006) 'The benefits and challenges of voluntary-academic sector partnerships: A critical reflection rooted in the Meleis criteria for culturally competent research', *Journal of Nursing Research*, 11 (6): 531–40.

Spencer, S. (2011) *Visual Research Methods in the Social Sciences*, Abingdon: Routledge.

Wiegman, R. (2012) *Object Lessons*. Durham, NC: Duke University Press.

Afterword

I am a migrant. After 15 years in Britain, I am now also a citizen but I insist on claiming the migrant label as a form of protest and a badge of pride. The ever intensifying anti-immigrant rhetoric and the expansion of border control into all areas of life, as part of the current government's hostile environment campaign, makes migrants like me feel that their citizenship is always conditional and their sense of belonging is fragile.

Getting indefinite leave to remain status meant that I was free from immigration control and gave me a sense of freedom. I felt free to protest against the injustices of the immigration system. I am ashamed that I waited until I felt 'safe'; many others in far more insecure situations speak out at great risk to themselves. But, like many others, I had kept my head down for years, anxiously monitoring Home Office pronouncements on immigration, trying to figure out how to stay ahead of a tightening net, navigating the uncertainty of finding out that you no longer qualify for the immigration category you're in. It felt like a finish line of sorts. Finally, I was home.

When I took up citizenship in 2013, the Go Home vans were already on London streets, ostensibly to encourage those who might be in the country illegally to return home. In reality, it felt like they were talking to all migrants, but especially ethnic minorities – regardless of immigration status – who had long heard the phrase 'Go Home' from the far right. For this message to be espoused so openly by the government of the day marked a turning point in how I viewed Britain and my citizenship. The message I heard was that while I held two homes in my heart, as far as this country was concerned, my right to claim this one would always be conditional.

During my citizenship ceremony I stood with people of all ages and experiences, each with their own stories of how they got here. For the first time I was told that my contribution to Britain mattered, that the vision for the country was for 'the common good'. My letter from the Home Secretary, who would go on to defend Operation Vaken and the Go Home vans in the face of criticism, told me for the first time that I was welcome, not far from one of the areas that the infamous van had been on tour.

The atmosphere in Britain at the moment does indeed feel hostile to migrants but its chill wind touches us all. Recent years have seen multiple Immigration Acts; no sooner had the 2015 Immigration Act passed than the Immigration Bill 2016 was being prepared. Yet despite the flurry of ever more restrictive legislation, public confidence in the immigration system does not improve and public anxieties about the level of immigration are not assuaged. Immigration critics like to say that we don't really talk about immigration but we talk of little else; the issue also underpins other debates – such as the EU referendum. Unease about immigration is expressed by politicians on behalf of 'the public'. In reality they are only listening and talking to one sector of the population. And instead of engaging with tangible concerns about services such as housing or living with difference and change, all too often they trade on fear with cheap gimmicks and soundbites, 'gesture politics' that give the impression of being tough on immigration.

However, it goes beyond crass stunts like the Go Home vans or staged immigration raids with the Prime Minister in tow. There are policies that undermine the rights of migrants and citizens alike. As the authors of this book show, the hostile environment campaign also entails the outsourcing of border control to private citizens such as landlords, doctors, teachers, lecturers – even the police, who under the newer Operation Nexus are forced to take a more active role in immigration enforcement, potentially jeopardising relationships with vulnerable groups and deterring those with insecure immigration status from seeking help. The media play their part in this 'performative politics' of immigration, sometimes reproducing, sometimes countering invasion imaginaries or the narrative that the UK is a soft touch when it comes to exploitation by certain migrants or 'bogus' asylum seekers. Media narratives reduce migrants to stereotypes – most often villains or victims, reinforcing the narrative of 'good' and 'bad' migrants and denying the complexity of life, which continually overspills neat immigration categories.

What does this do to us? Despite the rush for headlines, policies and publicity stunts, there is scant reflection on what this performative politics means for communities, for migrants and British citizens alike. This body of research is a timely and vital exploration of the changing face of immigration control, government communication campaigns and their effects.

Migration is not just about a journey; it is also the story of settlement – be it for a little while or a lifetime. Infrequent tabloid stories about the children of foreign-born parents sometimes label them as migrants despite the fact that most, along with their parents, will be British citizens. When do we get to belong? Who gets to decide? Is it dependent on the right paperwork? These are some of the questions that underlie the research discussed in this book.

In this context, for people like me reclaiming the undesirable label of migrant is an act of resistance. It shouldn't have to be. But this is one of many effects of the contemporary immigration debate and policy; the many strands of which are unpicked in this research. The lives and rights of migrants and citizens are more entwined than ever; where migrant rights are eroded, so are those of the most vulnerable British-born. Resistance requires solidarity, breaking out of the artificial categories that immigration legislation puts us in. After all, Britain's story is one of migration. The gesture politics mobilised for the purposes of immigration control, not only mystify the past, they are a failure of imagination and courage.

Kiri Kankhwende is a freelance journalist and commentator on immigration and politics and a member of Media Diversified.

Appendix: Further details on research methods

What we aimed to do

Our research began in 2013, with the following aims:

- to document high-profile Home Office campaigns against irregular immigration, in six local areas of the UK and at a national level
- to identify how government communications on migration interact with public debate and activism
- to produce analysis that informs debates, community action and policy, and that is useful to community organisations
- to develop new research methodologies that link digital, face-to-face and 'traditional' communications and policy channels
- to evaluate the effectiveness of the research and dissemination methodologies used in the project, and the project's impact.

Our research questions

We wanted to investigate these main questions:

What are the impacts of the Home Office high-profile publicity campaigns about migration? How are the messages of these government campaigns understood by residents in targeted areas? What forms of activism and community organising are being developed in response to these campaigns?

What are the relationships between public attitudes to 'illegal' migration, migration policy, racism and good community relations, particularly in a context of austerity? Who is aware of the government campaigns and activist responses to them? What are the class, ethnicity and gender dimensions of public debates at a UK level on migration? Do these differ at a local level? What is the role of social research in this?

What we did

Our qualitative research was based in six places: Barking and Dagenham; Bradford; Cardiff; Glasgow; Ealing and Hounslow; West Midlands (Birmingham and Coventry). Some of these (Barking and Dagenham, Ealing and Hounslow) were targeted by the Go Home vans. Others (Glasgow, Ealing and Hounslow) included reporting centres for migrants where similar advertising was used. All of the areas had experienced high-profile immigration raids; immigration had been covered in local news items with reporters accompanying border agents; signs about the limitation of migrant rights were displayed in public places (such as hospitals); and/or the areas had been involved in national debates about race and migration.

Across these areas, we conducted 13 focus groups with 67 people (including new migrants, long-settled migrants, ethnic minority and white British citizens), to understand the local effects of government campaigns on immigration. We also interviewed 24 local activists about the effects of Operation Vaken and other immigration enforcement initiatives on their work, and we spent time documenting local events and protests.

Nationally, we interviewed policy-makers about the intentions and thinking behind such campaigns (one MP, five civil servants located in Treasury, Business Innovation and Skills, Home Office and three people from Westminster think tanks) and attended two Westminster roundtables discussing immigration, organised by think tanks and lobby groups.

We also commissioned a survey from Ipsos MORI to investigate awareness and reactions to the government campaigns. Questions were placed on the Ipsos MORI Omnibus (Capibus) amongst a nationally representative quota sample of 2,424 adults (aged 15 and over). Within this, a total of 580 black and minority ethnic individuals were interviewed. Interviews were conducted face-to-face in peoples' homes between 15 August and 9 September 2014, using Computer Assisted Personal Interviewing software. All data are weighted to the known national profile of adults aged 15+ in Great Britain.

As the project got under way, we participated in and documented online debates about key elements of the campaigns and reactions to them. We took our interim findings back to the communities and organisations with whom we had done the initial research, and included their responses in the findings.

From the outset of the project we worked with community organisations as partners. This helped to guide the direction of the research, ensuring that it had some value and relevance beyond academia, and that it also included invaluable practical research support. Through the project we hoped to unsettle or at least bring into question the division between 'activism' and 'academia'. We tried to think carefully about the sort of contributions academic researchers can make to the groups and individuals we work with – because of the time, resources and specialist skills to which we have access – and to recognise that research partners and participants may have similar skills but are in different situations during the project, because of their personal circumstances, political commitments, institutional priorities, or pressures of time, workload and resources. In being able to attach funds to the work done by the community partners, we could recognise and value their expertise and time commitment to the project.

Such partnership working took place in a context where there are immense pressures on the voluntary sector. We were very conscious of adding to the workload of these groups. Therefore being clear about roles within the project and managing expectations on both sides was crucial. In addition, for groups working on asylum issues with specific goals there was sometimes a mismatch between our interests (anti-immigration campaigns) and the very specific and urgent issues groups were dealing with (such as destitution and deportation). This is an ongoing question, which needs to be continuously negotiated in research projects like ours.

Index